THE STORY OF

CAWNPORE

BY CAPTAIN MOWBRAY THOMPSON,
ONE OF THE ONLY TWO SURVIVORS
FROM THE CAWNPORE GARRISON.

FOLLETT, FOSTER & CO.,
1859

From "The Heroes of the Indian Rebellion"

By D. W. Bartlett

Table of Contents

Cover: "Massacre in the boats off Cawnpore" from - *The History of the Indian Mutiny* by Charles Ball 1859

CAWNPORE – BEFORE.

In December, 1856, my regiment, the 53d Native Infantry, was ordered to Cawnpore. The 53d Native Infantry was a fine regiment, about a thousand strong, almost all of them Oude men, averaging five feet, eight inches in height; their uniform the old British red, with yellow facings. By far the greater number of them being high caste men, they were regarded by the native populace as very aristocratic and stylish gentlemen, and yet their pay would sound to English ears as any thing but compatible with the height of gentility, namely, seven rupees a man per month, out of which exorbitant sum they provided all their own food, and a suit of summer clothing. Be astonished, ye beef eating Guardsmen! The greater number of these swarthy Sepoys were able to defray all the cost of their food with three rupees each a month. Thoroughly disciplined and martial in appearance, these native troops presented one memorable point of contrast with European forces, drunkenness was altogether unknown among them.

The city of Cawnpore, which has obtained such a painful notoriety in connection with the mutiny of 1857, is distant from Calcutta 628 miles by land, 954 by water, and 266 miles southeast from Delhi; it is the principal town in the district of the Doab formed by the Ganges and the Jumna, and is situated on the right bank of the queen of the Indian rivers. At the period of the dismemberment of the Mogul empire this district passed into the hands of the Nawaub of Oude.

By the treaty of Fyzabad, in 1775, the East India Company engaged to supply a brigade for the defense of the frontiers of Oude, and Cawnpore was selected as the station for that force; a subsidy being paid by the protected country for the maintenance of the troops. Subsequently, in 1801, Lord Wellesley commuted this payment for the surrender of the district to the Company's territory, and thus gained an important barrier against the threatened invasion of the south, from Cabul and Afghanistan. Cawnpore immediately rose into one of the most important of the Company's garrisons.

The cantonments, which are quite distinct from the native city, are spread over an extent of six miles, in a semicircular form, along the bank of the river, and contain an area of ten square miles. Hundreds of bungalows, the residences of the officers, stand in the midst of gardens, and these interspersed with forest trees, the barracks of the troops, with a separate bazar for each regiment, and the canvas town of the tented regiments, give to the *tout ensemble* a picturesque effect as seen from the river. On the highest ground in the cantonments stand the church and the assembly rooms; in another part a theater, in which amateur performances were occasionally given; and a cafe supported by public subscription. In the officers' gardens, which were among the best in India, most kinds of European vegetables thrived, while peaches, melons, mangoes, shaddocks, limes, oranges, plantains, guavas, and custard apples were abundant. Fish, flesh, and fowl are always plentiful, and in the season for game, quails, snipes, and wild ducks can be had cheap enough. The ortolan, which in Europe is the gourmand's despair, during the hot winds, is seen in such dense flights that fifty or sixty might be brought down at a shot. In winter the temperature falls low enough to freeze water, which for this purpose is exposed in shallow earthen pans, and then collected into capacious ice houses, to furnish the exotic residents with the luxury so indispensable to their comfort during the hot season, when this becomes one of the hottest stations in India. Besides all these indigenous supplies, the far traveling spirit of commerce is not unmindful of the numerous personal wants which John Bull carries with him all the world over. In the cold season, boating and horse racing were the diversions most patronized by the officers; *au reste*, drill, parade, and regimental orders, varied by an occasional court martial upon some swarthy delinquent, mails home and mails from home, morning calls, and evening dinners, formed the chief avocations of all seasons.

The breadth of the Ganges at Cawnpore, in the dry

season, is about five hundred yards, but when the rains have filled up its bed it becomes more than a mile across. Navigable for light craft downward to the sea 1,000 miles, and up the country 300 miles, the scene which the river presents is full of life and variety; at the ghant, or landing place, a busy trade is constantly plying. A bridge of boats constructed by the Government, and for the passage of which a toll is charged, serves to conduct a ceaseless throng over into Oude. Merchants, travelers, fakirs, camels, bullocks, horses, go and come incessantly. Moored inshore are multitudes of vessels, looking with their thatched roofs like a floating village, while down the stream the pinnace with her thin, light masts and tight rigging, the clumsy looking budgerow with its stern high above the bows, and the country boats like drifting stacks, with their crews rowing, singing, and smoking, give such a diversity to the scene as no other river can boast. The great Trunk Road which passes close by the city, brings up daily relays of travelers and detachments of troops to the northward, all of whom halt at Cawnpore, and the railroad, which is now complete from Allahabad, will yet further enhance the busy traffic at this station. The cantonments have not infrequently contained as many as 6,000 troops, and these increased by the crowd of camp followers, have made the population of the military bazars 50,000 in number.

The native city is densely packed and closely built as all the human hives of the east are, and it contained at the time of the mutiny about 60,000 inhabitants. It has only one good avenue, which may be called its Broadway, the Chandneechoke. This street is about three hundred yards long and thirty five yards in breadth, and is filled with the shops of saddlers, silk merchants, and dealers in the fine fabrics and cunning workmanship in gold and silver, that from time immemorial have attracted western barbarians to the splendid commerce of the east. The principal productions of the city are, however, saddlery and shoes, the former of which is especially popular throughout India for its excellence and cheapness; a set of good single horse driving harness costs from twenty five to fifty shillings, and the equestrian can equip himself luxuriantly with bridle, saddle, etc., for thirty shillings. Country horses, as they are called, sell for about a hundred rupees, but Arabs brought down the Persian Gulf and across from Bombay are the chief favorites, and command a high price.

At the period with which this narrative commences, the following regiments constituted the force occupying the Cawnpore garrison: the 1st, 53d, and 56th Native Infantry; the 2d Cavalry, and a company of artillerymen, all of these being Sepoys, and about 3,000 in number.

The European residents consisted of the officers

attached to the Sepoy regiments; 60 men of the 84th Regiment; 74 men of the 32d Regiment, who were invalided; 15 men of the Madras Fusileers, and 59 men of the Company's Artillery, about 300 combatants in all. In addition to these there were the wives, children, and native servants of the officers; 300 half caste children belonging to the Cawnpore school; merchants, some Europeans and others Eurasians, shopkeepers, railway officials, and their families. Some of the civilians at the station were permanently located there, others had escaped from disturbances in the surrounding districts; the entire company included considerably more than a thousand Europeans.

General Sir Hugh Wheeler, K. C. B., was the commandant of the division, and Mr. Hillersden the magistrate of the Cawnpore district.

The first intimation that appeared of any disaffection in the minds of the natives was the circulation of chupatties and lotus leaves. Early in March it was reported that a chowkedar, or village policeman, of Cawnpore, had run up to one of his comrades and had given him two chupatties. These are unleavened cakes made of flour, water, and salt; the mode of telegraphing by their means was for the cakes to be eaten in the presence of the giver, and fresh ones made by the newly initiated one, who in his turn distributed them to new candidates for participation in the mystery. The chupatties were limited to civilians; and lotus leaves, the emblem of war, were in like manner handed about among the soldiery. Various speculations were made by Europeans as to the import of this extreme activity in the circulation of these occult harbingers of the mutiny, but they subsided into an impression that they formed some portion of the native superstitions. And no one dreamed, like the man in Gideon's camp, who saw the barley cake overturn the tents of Midian, that these farinaceous weapons were aimed at the overthrow of the British rule in India.

Upon the 14th of May intelligence reached us of the revolt at Meerut and the subsequent events at Delhi; but no apprehension was felt of treachery on the part of our own troops. A few Sepoys, who had been for instruction to the school of musketry at Umballa, returned to their respective regiments, and they were amicably received, and allowed to eat with their own caste, although they had been using the Enfield rifle and the suspected cartridges. One of these men, Mhan Khan, a Mussulman private of the 53d, brought with him specimens of the cartridges, to assure his comrades that no animal fat had been employed in their construction. It may be as well to state that the first installment of these notorious cartridges, which were sent out from England, and intended for the use of the Queen's troops, were, without doubt, abundantly offensive to the Feringhees as well as to the faithful, and from the nauseous odor which accompanied them quite equal to breeding a pestilence, if not adequate to the task which has been attributed to them of causing the mutiny.

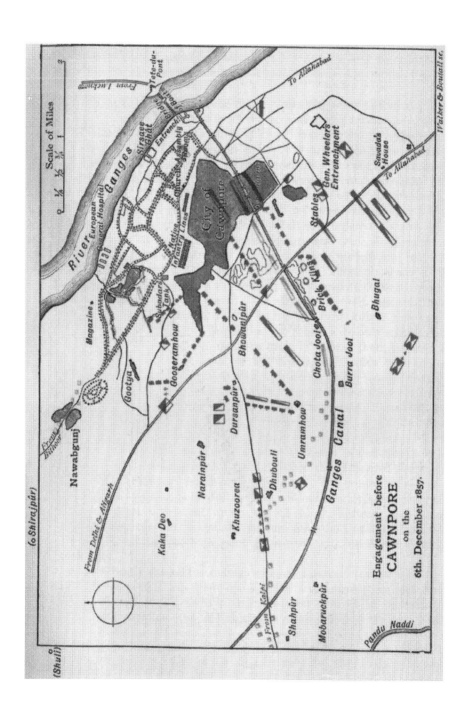

Engagement before
CAWNPORE
on the
6th. December 1857.

9

THE MUTINY.

Two or three days after the arrival of the tidings from Delhi of the massacre which had been perpetrated in the old city of the Moguls, Mrs. Fraser, the wife of an officer in the 27th Native Infantry, reached our cantonments, having traveled from that scene of bloodshed and revolt. The native driver, who had taken her up in the precincts of the city, brought her faithfully to the end of her hazardous journey of two hundred and sixty six miles. The exposure which she had undergone was evident from a bullet that had pierced the carriage. Her flight from Delhi was but the beginning of the sorrows of this unfortunate lady, though she deserves rather to be commemorated for her virtues than her sufferings. During the horrors of the siege she won the admiration of all our party by her indefatigable attentions to the wounded. Neither danger nor fatigue seemed to have power to suspend her ministry of mercy. Even on the fatal morning of embarkation, although she had escaped to the boats with scarcely any clothing upon her, in the thickest of the deadly volleys poured upon us from the banks, she appeared alike indifferent to danger and to her own scanty covering; while, with perfect equanimity and imperturbed fortitude, she was entirely occupied in the attempt to soothe and relieve the agonized sufferers around her, whose wounds scarcely made their condition worse than her own. Such rare heroism deserves a far higher tribute than this simple record from my pen; but I feel a mournful satisfaction in publishing a fact which a more experienced scribe would have depicted in language more worthy of the subject, though not with admiration or regret deeper or more sincere than that which I feel. Mrs. Fraser was one of the party recaptured from the boats, and is reported to have died from fever before the terrific butchery that immediately preceded General Havelock's recapture of Cawnpore.

About the 20th of May intelligence came that all communications with Delhi were now entirely suspended. The road northward was infested with dacoits and liberated convicts, and all Europeans traveling in that direction were compelled to tarry in our cantonments. Our parades still continued with their accustomed regularity; no suspicion was uttered, if entertained, of the fidelity of our Sepoys, although serious apprehension began to be felt of the probability of an attack from without, more especially as we were known to be in possession of a considerable amount of Government treasure.

The Mohammedan festival of the Eede passed off quietly, and the Mussulmans gave the salaam to their officers, and assured us that, come what would, they would stand faithfully to their leaders. A fire broke out in the lines of the 1st

11

Native Infantry in the night of the 20th, which was supposed to be the work of an incendiary, and the probable signal for revolt; six guns were accordingly run down to a preconcerted place of rendezvous, and the Sepoys were ordered to extinguish the flames; this was done promptly, and the cause of the fire was found to have been accidental. Day after day news came of the growth of the storm. Etawah and Allyghurh, both towns between Delhi and Cawnpore, were plundered, and the insurgents were reported as enroute for Cawnpore. The sergeant-major's wife of the 53d, an Eurasian by birth, went marketing to the native bazar, when she was accosted by a Sepoy out of regimental dress, "You will none of you come here much oftener; you will not be alive another week." She reported her story at headquarters, but it was thought advisable to discredit the tale. Several of us at this period endeavored to persuade the ladies to leave the station and retreat to Calcutta for safety; but they unanimously declined to remove so long as General Wheeler retained his family with him.

Determined, self possessed, and fearless of danger, Sir Hugh Wheeler now made arrangements for the protection of the women and children. A mud wall, four feet high, was thrown up round the old dragoon hospital. The buildings thus intrenched were two brick structures, one thatched, the other roofed with masonry. On the 21st of May the women and children were all ordered into these barracks, the officers still sleeping at the quarter-guards in the lines with their respective corps. Around the intrenchments the guns were placed, three on the northeast side commanding the lines, and three on the south to range the plain which separates the cantonments from the city. A small three-pounder, which had been rifled by Lieutenant Fosbury a year or two before, was also brought into use, and placed so as to command the new barracks which were in course of erection; this piece, however, could only be used for grape, as there was no conical shot in store. A few days afterward, Lieutenant Ashe, of the Bengal Artillery, arrived from Lucknow with a half battery, consisting of two nine-pounders and one twenty-four-pounder howitzer. . . . At length the much dreaded explosion came. On the night of the 6th of June the 2d Cavalry broke out. They first set fire to the riding master's bungalow, and then fled, carrying off with them horses, arms, colors, and the regimental treasure chest. The old soubhadar-major of the regiment defended the colors and treasure, which were in the quarter-guard, as long as he could, and the poor old fellow was found in the morning severely wounded, and lying in his blood at his post. This was the only instance of any native belonging to that regiment who retained his fidelity. The old man remained with us, and was killed by a shell in the intrenchment. An hour or two after the flight of the cavalry, the 1st Native Infantry also bolted, leaving their officers untouched upon the parade ground. The 56th Native Infantry followed the next morning. The 53d remained, till, by some error of the General, they were fired into. I am at an utter loss to account for this proceeding. The men were peacefully occupied in their lines, cooking; no signs of mutiny had appeared amidst their ranks; they had refused all the solicitations of the deserters to accompany them, and seemed quite steadfast, when Ashe's battery opened upon them by Sir Hugh Wheeler's command, and they were literally driven from us by nine-pounders. The only signal that had preceded this step was the calling in to the intrenchments of the native officers of the regiment. The whole of them cast in their lot with us, besides a hundred and fifty privates, most of them belonging to the Grenadier company. The detachment of the 53d, posted at the treasury, held their ground against the rebels about four hours. We could hear their musketry in the distance, but were not allowed to attempt their relief. The faithful little band that had joined our desperate fortunes was ordered to occupy the military hospital, about six hundred yards to the east of our position, and they held it for nine days, when, in consequence of its being set on fire, they were compelled to evacuate. They applied for admission to the intrenchments, but were told that we had not food sufficient to allow of an increase to our number. Major Hillersden gave them a few rupees each, together with a certificate of their fidelity. Had it been possible to have received these men, they would have constituted a powerful addition to our force, just as the few gallant remnants of the native regiments at Lucknow did throughout the second edition of the Cawnpore siege, as it was enacted in the Oude capital.

The name most familiarly associated with the events of the mutiny is that borne by a man whose history is almost unknown out of India. And as Nana Sahib will always be identified with the sanguinary proceedings at Cawnpore, it will not be out of place to give the reader some idea of the antecedents of this notorious scoundrel. Seereek Dhoondoo Punth, or, as he is now universally called, the Nana, that is, grandson, and by the majority of newspaper readers Nana Sahib, is the adopted son of the late Bajee Rao, who was Peishaw of Poonah, and the last of the Mahratta kings. Driven by his faithlessness and uncontrollable treachery to dethrone the old man, the British Government assigned him a residence at Bithoor, twelve miles from Cawnpore, where he dwelt till his death in 1851, at a safe distance from all Mahratta associations, but, as to his own personal condition, in most sumptuous and right regal splendor. Bajee Rao was sonless, a deplorable condition in the estimation of a Brahmin prince; he, therefore, had recourse to adoption, and Seereek Dhoondoo Punth was the favored individual of his selection. Some say that the Nana is really the son of a corn dealer of Poonah; others, that he is the offspring of a poor Konkanee Brahmin, and that he first saw the light at Venn, a miserable little village about thirty miles east of Bombay. Shortly after the death of Bajee Rao, the Nana presented a claim upon the East India Company for a continuance of the pension allowed to the old Mahratta. As the allowance made to the king was purely in the form of an annuity, the demand of the heir to all his private property to enjoy a share of the Indian revenue was most emphatically denied. Hence the vigorous venom which he imparted to the enterprise of the mutineers. It is always a matter of difficulty to decide upon the exact age of an Asiatic, but I should consider the Nana to be about thirty six years old. With greater confidence I can add, that he is extremely corpulent, of sallow complexion, of middle light, with thoroughly marked features, and, like all Mahrattas, clean shaven on both head and face. He does not speak a word of English.

Bithoor palace, which he inherited from his benefactor, is a well situated town. It has several Hindoo temples, and ghauts, which give access to the sacred stream. Brahma is specially reverenced here. At the principal ghaut he is said to have offered an aswamedha on completing the act of creation.

The pin of his slipper, left behind him on the occasion, is fastened into one of the steps of the ghaut, and is the object of worship. There is an annual gathering to this spot at the full moon of November, which attracts prodigious numbers of devotees, and contributes quite as much to the prosperity of the town as it does to the piety of the pilgrims. The palace was spacious, and though not remarkable for any architectural beauty, was exquisitely furnished in European style. All the reception rooms were decorated with immense mirrors and massive chandeliers in variegated glass, and of the most recent manufacture: the floor was covered with the finest productions of the Indian looms, and all the appurtenances of eastern splendor were strewed about in prodigious abundance. There were saddles of silver for both horses and camels, guns of every possible construction, shields inlaid with gold, carriages for camel driving, and the newest turn outs from Long Acre; plate, gems, and curiosities in ivory and metal; while without in the compound might be seen the fleetest horses, the finest dogs, and rare specimens of deer, antelopes, and other animals from all parts of India. It would be quite impossible to lift the vail that must rest on the private life of this man. There were apartments in the Bithoor palace horribly unfit for any human eye; in which both European and native artists had done their utmost to gratify the corrupt master, from whom they could command any price.

It was frequently the custom of the Nana to entertain the officers of the Cawnpore garrison in the most sumptuous style; although he would accept none of their hospitality in return, because no salute was permitted in his honor. I have been a guest in those halls when costly festivities were provided for the very persons who were at length massacred by their quondam host; and I was there also when Havelock's Ironsides gave their entertainment, shattering to powder all that was fragile, in revenge for the atrocities lying unrequited at those doors. For downright looting commend me to the hirsute Sikh; for destructive aggression, battering, and but-ending, the palm must be awarded to the privates of Her Britannic Majesty's _____ Regiment. "Look what I have found!" said a too demonstrative individual of the last named corps, at the same time holding up a bag full of rupees for the gaze of his comrades, when an expert Sikh with a blow of his tulwar cut the canvas that held the treasure, and sent the glittering spoil flying among the eager spectators.

A large portion of the Nana's plate was found in the wells around the palace; gold dishes, some of them as much as two feet in diameter; silver jugs; spittoons of both gold and silver, that had been used by the betel eating Brahmin, were fished up, and proved glorious prizes for somebody. Every cranny in the house was explored, floors were removed, partitions pulled down, and every square foot on the surface of the adjacent grounds pierced and dug in the search after spoil. Brazier's Sikhs have the credit of carrying off Bajee Rao's state sword, which, in consequence of its magnificent setting in jewels, is said to have been worth at least thirty thousand pounds. The most portable of his riches the Nana carried with him in his flight. The natives say that immediately before the insurrection at Meerut he sold out seventy lacs of government paper, £70,000. One ruby of great size and brilliancy he is alleged to have sold recently for ten thousand rupees to a native banker; the tradition is, that he carried this gem continually about his person, intending, should he be driven to extremities, to destroy himself by swallowing it; a curious mode of suicide, the efficacy of which I am not prepared either to dispute or to defend; my informant told me that the sharp edges of the ruby would cut through the vitals, and speedily destroy life. The Nana's dignity was enhanced by the presence of a few hundred armed retainers, with whom he played the rajah; the pay of each of these men was four rupees a month and a suit of clothes per annum, foraging performed on their own account. It would have been quite a work of supererogation for the Oude and Mahratta princes to have fed their troops, as they always knew where to find copious supplies at a nominal price. Their perpetual rapine made them a curse to the poor ryots, who were never safe from their extortions and pillage.

The only Englishman resident at Bithoor was a Mr. Todd, who had come out in the employment of the Grand Trunk railroad, but for some reason had exchanged his situation for that of teacher of English to the household of his Excellency Seereek Dhoondoo Punth. Mr. Todd was allowed to join us in the intrenchment; when the siege began he was appointed to my picket, and was one of those who perished at the time of embarkation.

The following little incident will serve to show the extreme servility of the most exalted of Hindoo potentates to the despotic sway of their spiritual guides. Once upon a time Seereek Dhondoo Punth had committed some peccadillo which had awakened all the indignation and abhorrence of his pundits and priests. Now it so fell out that at the same time, or sufficiently, near about thereto for the object of their holinesses, the capricious Ganges, having formed a sand bank under the walls of Bithoor, was diverted from its ancient course, so as to threaten the Residency with a scarcity of water. The priests persuaded their devotee that this was a visitation consequent upon his sin, and implored him, as he valued his own life and that of his peasantry, to propitiate the sacred stream. The offering proposed was to be pecuniary; the amount, one lac of rupees; the mode of presentation, casting them into the bed of the river; the period, an early date chosen by lot. These cautious and speculative gentlemen forthwith proceeded to underlay the waters with some good, stout sail cloth; at the appointed time they indicated the precise spot at which only the offering could be efficacious: this also, no doubt, was chosen by lot. The Nana, in great state, made his costly libation, and somebody removed the sail cloth; but, alas! the Ganges did not return.

When Havelock's force paid their first visit to Bithoor, they found the place deserted, but the guns in position and loaded. This is said to have been done by Narrein Rao, the son of the old Mahratta's Commander-in-chief. This man welcomed the English troops on their arrival, and alleged that he had pointed the guns as a feint to make the rebels believe that he was about to attack General Havelock's advancing columns. Certain it is that this man and the Nana had always been in hot water. Narrein Rao very energetically sided with the General; he found supplies and horses for the police. It seems decidedly more than probable that the lion's share of the Bithoor valuables fell to Narrein, as he was conveniently on the spot when the retreaters evacuated, and had the additional advantage of knowing better where to look for things than the inexperienced fresh arrivals did. I must not, however, speak to the disparagement of this gentleman, because when I left Cawnpore for England, he presented me with a fine pearl ring as a proof of the esteem in which he is pleased to hold me; some persons might think its intrinsic value increased because it once adorned the Nana's hand.

Less known in England by report, though better known by virtue of personal acquaintance, and a far more remarkable individual than the Nana, is he who bears the name, Azimoolah Khan. This man's adventures are of the kind, for their numerous transitions and mysterious alternations, that belong only to eastern story. I can easily imagine that the bare mention of his name will have power sufficient to cause some trepidation and alarm to a few of my fair readers; but I will betray no confidences. Read on, my lady, no names shall be divulged, only should some unpleasant recollection of our hero's fascination be called to mind, let them serve as a warning against the too confiding disposition which once betrayed you into a hasty admiration of this swarthy adventurer. Azimoolah was originally a khitmutghar, waiter at table, in some Anglo-Indian family; profiting by the opportunity thus afforded him, he acquired a thorough acquaintance with the English and French languages, so as to be able to read and converse fluently, and write accurately in them both. He afterward became a pupil, and subsequently a teacher, in the Cawnpore government schools, and from the last named position he was selected to become the vakeel, or prime agent, of the Nana. On account of his numerous qualifications he was deputed to visit England, and press upon the authorities in Leadenhall street the application for the continuance of Bajee Rao's pension.

Azimoolah accordingly reached London in the season of 1854. Passing himself off as an Indian prince, and being thoroughly furnished with ways and means, and having withal a most presentable contour, he obtained admission to distinguished society. In addition to the political business which he had in hand, he was at one time prosecuting a suit of his own of a more delicate character; but, happily for our fair countrywoman, who was the object of his attentions, her friends interfered and saved her from becoming an item in the harem of this Mohammedan polygamist. Foiled in all his attempts to obtain the pension for his employer, he returned to India via France; and report says that he there renewed his endeavors to form a European alliance for his own individual benefit. I believe that Azimoolah took the way of Constantinople also on his homeward route. Howbeit this was just at the time when prospects were gloomy in the Crimea, and the opinion was actually promulgated throughout the continental nations that the struggle with Russia had crippled the resources, and humbled the high crest of England; and by some it was thought she would henceforth be scarcely able to hold her own against bolder and abler hands. Doubtless the wish was father to the thought. It is matter of notoriety that such vaticinations as these were at the period in question current from Calais to Cairo, and it is not unlikely that the poor comfort Azimoolah could give the Nana, in reporting on his unsuccessful journey, would be in some measure compensated for, by the tidings that the Feringhees were ruined, and that one decisive blow would destroy their yoke in the east. I believe that the mutiny had its origin in the diffusion of such statements at Delhi, Lucknow, and other teeming cities in India. Subtle, intriguing, politic, unscrupulous, and bloodthirsty, sleek and wary as a tiger, this man betrayed no animosity to us till the outburst of the mutiny, and then he became the presiding genius in the assault on Cawnpore. I regret that his name does not appear, as it certainly ought to have done, upon the list of outlaws published by the Governor-General; for this Azimoolah was the actual murderer of our sisters and their babes. When Havelock's men cleared out Bithoor, they found most expressive traces of the success he had obtained in his ambitious pursuit of distinction in England, in the shape of letters from titled ladies couched in the terms of most courteous friendship. Little could they have suspected the true character of their honored correspondent.

On one occasion, shortly after the report of the *emeute* at Meerut had reached us, Azimoolah met Lieutenant M. G. Daniell, of our garrison, and said to him, pointing toward our intrenched barrack:

"What do you call that place you are making out in the plain?"

"I am sure I don't know," was the reply. Azimoolah suggested it should be named the fort of despair.

"No," said Daniell; "we will call it the fort of victory." "Aha! aha!" replied the wily eastern, with a silent sneer that betrayed the lurking mischief.

Lieutenant Daniell had been a great favorite at Bithoor; on one occasion the Nana took off a valuable diamond ring from his own hand, and gave it to him, as a present. Poor Daniell survived the siege, but was wounded in my boat, during the embarkation, by a musket shot in the temple, but whether he perished in the river, or was carried back to Cawnpore, I can not say; he was quite young, scarcely of age, but brave to admiration, a fearless horseman, foremost in all field sports, and universally beloved for his great amiability. On one occasion during the siege, while we were making a sortie to clear the adjacent barracks of some of our assailants, Daniell and I heard sounds of struggling in a room close at hand; rushing in together, we saw Captain Moore, our second in command, lying on the ground under the grasp of a powerful native, who was on the point of cutting the Captain's throat. A fall from his horse a few days previously, resulting in a broken collarbone, had disabled Moore, and rendered him unequal to such an encounter; he would certainly have been killed had not Daniell's bayonet instantly transfixed the Sepoy.

Early on the morning of Sunday the 7th of June, all the officers were called into the intrenchments, in consequence of the reception of a letter by Sir Hugh Wheeler from the Nana, in which he declared his intention of at once attacking us. With such expedition was the summons obeyed, that we were compelled to leave all our goods and chattels to fall a prey to the ravages of the Sepoys; and after they had appropriated all movables of value they set fire to the bungalows. While in happy England the Sabbath bells were ringing, in the day of peace and rest, we were in suspense peering over our mud wall at the destructive flames that were consuming all our possessions, and expecting the more dreaded fire that was to be aimed at the persons of hundreds of women and children about us. Very few of our number had secured a single change of raiment; some, like myself, were only partially dressed, and even in the beginning of our defense, we were like a band of seafarers who had taken to a raft to escape their burning ship. Upon my asking Brigadier Jack if I might run to the café for some refreshment, he informed me that the General's order was most peremptory that not a soul should be permitted to leave our quarters, as the attack was momentarily expected. In the course of a short time the whole of the men capable of bearing arms were called together, and told off in batches under their respective officers. A reference to the plan of the position, will enable the reader to understand the following details of the defense:

On the north, Major Vibart of the 2d Cavalry, assisted by Captain Jenkins, held the Redan, which was an earthwork defending the whole of the northern side. At the northeast battery, Lieutenant Ashe, of the Oude Irregular Artillery, commanded one twenty-four-pounder howitzer and two nine-pounders, assisted by Lieutenant Sotheby. Captain Kempland, 56th Native Infantry, was posted on the south side. Lieutenant Eckford, of the Artillery, had charge of the southeast battery with three nine-pounders, assisted by Lieutenant Burney, also of the Artillery, and Lieutenant Delafosse, of the 53d Native Infantry. The main guard, from south to west, was held by Lieutenant Turnbull, 13th Native Infantry. On the west, Lieutenant C. Dempster commanded three nine-pounders, assisted by Lieutenant Martin. Flanking the west battery the little rifled three-pounder was stationed, with a detachment under the command of Major Front, 56th Native Infantry; and on the northwest Captain Whiting held the command. The general command of the artillery was given to Colonel Larkins, but in consequence of the shattered state of that officer's health, he was able to take but a small part in the defense. At each of the batteries, infantry were posted fifteen paces apart, under the cover of the mud wall, four feet in height; this service was shared by combatants and noncombatants alike, without any relief; each man had at least three loaded muskets by his side, with bayonet fixed in case of assault; but in most instances our trained men had as many as seven, and even eight muskets each. The batteries were none of them masked or fortified in any way, and the gunners were in consequence exposed to a most murderous fire. It will be seen in the plan of the siege that a number of barracks running up from the Allahabad Road commanded our intrenchments. On this account a detachment of our limited force was placed in one of them. They consisted chiefly of civil engineers who had been connected with the railway works. The whole of these arrangements for the defense were made by General Wheeler and Captain Moore, of Her Majesty's 32d Foot.

As soon as all these positions had been occupied, Lieutenant Ashe, with about twenty or thirty volunteers, took his guns out to reconnoiter, as we heard the sound of the approaching foe. After going out about five hundred yards, they caught sight of the enemy, in possession of one of the canal bridges, close by the lines of the 1st Native Infantry. They came back at a trot into the intrenchment; but Lieutenant Ashburner, who was one of the number, was never seen or heard of again. It was supposed that his horse bolted with him into the Sepoy ranks, and that he was cut up by them instantly. Mr. Murphy, who had been attached to the railway corps, went out of the intrenchments and came back severely wounded by a musket ball; he died the same day, and was the only one of our slain buried in a coffin, one having been found in the hospital. This gentleman, and Mrs. Wade, who died of fever, were the only persons interred inside the intrenchment. Shortly after the return of Lieutenant Ashe, the first shot fired by the mutineers came from a nine-pounder, on the northwest; it struck the crest of the mud wall and glided over into the puckah roofed barrack. This was about 10 o'clock, A. M.; a large party of ladies and children were outside the barrack; the consternation caused among them was indescribable; the bugle call sent every man of us instantly to his post, many of us carrying in our ears, for the first time, the peculiar whizzing of round shot, with which we were to become so familiar. As the day advanced the enemy's fire grew hotter and more dangerous, in consequence of their getting the guns into position. The first casualty occurred at the west battery; M'Guire, a gunner, being killed by a round shot; the poor fellow was covered with a blanket and left in the trench till nightfall. Several of us saw the ball bounding toward us, and he also evidently saw it, but, like many others whom I saw fall at different times, he seemed fascinated to the spot. All through this first weary day the shrieks of the women and children were terrific; as often as the balls struck the walls of the barracks their wailings were heart rending, but after the initiation of that first day, they had learned silence, and never uttered a sound except when groaning from the horrible mutilations they had to endure.

When night sheltered them, our cowardly assailants closed in upon the intrencbments, and harassed us with incessant volleys of musketry. Waiting the assault that we supposed to be impending, not a man closed his eyes in sleep, and throughout the whole siege, snatches of troubled slumber under the cover of the wall, was all the relief the combatants could obtain. The ping ping of rifle bullets would break short dreams of home or of approaching relief, pleasant visions made horrible by waking to the state of things around; and if it were so with men of mature years, sustained by the fullness of physical strength, how much more terrific were the nights passed inside those barracks by our women and children! As often as the shout of our sentinels was heard, each half hour sounding the "All's well," the spot from which the voice proceeded became the center for hundreds of bullets. At different degrees of distance, from fifty to four hundred yards and more, they hovered about during the hours of darkness, always measuring the range by daylight, and then pouring in from under the cover of adjacent buildings or ruins of buildings, the fire of their artillery, or rather of our artillery turned against us. The execution committed by the twenty-four-pounders they had was terrific, though they were not always a match for the devices we adopted to divert their aim. When we wanted to create a diversion, we used to pile up some of the muskets behind the mud wall, and mount them with hats and shakos, and then allow the Sepoys to expend their powder on these dummies, while we went elsewhere.

But if the intrenched position was one of peril, that of the out-picket in barrack No. 4 was even more so. The railway gentlemen held this post for three entire days, without any military superintendence whatever, and they distinguished themselves greatly by their skill and courage. I remember particularly Messrs. Heberden, Latouche, and Miller, as prominent in the midst of these undisciplined soldiers for their eminently good service. Their sharp sight and accurate knowledge of distances acquired in surveying, had made these gentlemen invaluable as marksmen, while still higher moral qualities constituted them an addition to our force not to be estimated by their numbers.

INCIDENTS OF THE SIEGE.

Our scanty dietary was occasionally improved by the addition of horse soup; a Brahminee bull was shot, but the question was how to get the carcass. Presently a volunteer party was formed to take this bull by the horns, no trifle, since the distance from the wall was full three hundred yards, and the project involved the certainty of encountering twice three hundred bullets. But beef was scarce, and led on by Captain Moore, eight or ten accordingly went out after the animal. They took with them a strong rope, fastened it round the hind legs and between the horns of the beast, and in the midst of the cheers from behind the mud wall, a sharp fusilade from the rebels, diversified with one or two round shots, they accomplished their object. Two or three ugly wounds were not thought too high a price to pay for this contribution to the commissariat. The costly bull was soon made into soup, but none of it reached us in the outposts more palpably than in its irritating odor. Sometimes, however, we in the outposts had meat when there was none at headquarters. We once saw the Sepoys bring up a nine-pounder to barrack No. 6, and great expectations were entertained that the half dozen artillery bullocks employed in that piece of service might by a little ingenuity, or at least some of them, be shortly transformed into stew on our behalf. Not a few of my men would have given a right arm for a good cut out of the sides, and not a few of their officers would have bartered a letter of credit on the army agents for the same privilege. But the pandies artfully kept the horned treasure under cover. We watched the ends of the distant walls in vain. Some of our famished Esaus would have made for the cannon's mouth, and have sold their lives, but it might not be; and our hungry disgust had well nigh sunk into despair, when an old knacker came into range, that had belonged to an Irregular Cavalryman. He was down by a shot like lightning, brought into the barrack, and hewn up. We did not wait to skin the prey, nor waste any time in consultation upon its anatomical arrangements; no scientific butchery was considered necessary in its subdivision. Lump, thump, whack, went nondescript pieces of flesh into the fire, and, notwithstanding its decided claims to veneration on the score of antiquity, we thought it a more savory meal than any of the *recherche* culinary curiosities of the lamented Soyer. The two pickets, thirty four in number, disposed of the horse in two meals. The head, and some mysteries of the body, we stewed into soup, and liberally sent to fair friends in the intrenchment, without designating its nature, or without being required to satisfy any scruples upon that head. Though, alas! death, which marked every event in our career, sealed this also, for Captain Halliday, who had come across to visit my neighbor, Captain Jenkins, was carrying back some of the said soup for his wife, when he was shot dead between the puckah barrack and the main guard. Further on in the history of the siege, when our privation was even greater than on the last occasion, a stray dog approached us. The cur had wandered from the Sepoy barrack, and every possible blandishment was employed by my men to tempt the canine adventurer into the soup kettle. Two or three minutes subsequently to my seeing him doubtfully trotting across the open, I was offered some of his semi roasted fabric, but that, more scrupulous than others, I was obliged to decline.

Our position behind these unroofed walls was one of intense suffering, in consequence of the unmitigated heat of the sun by day, and the almost perpetual surprises to which we were liable by night.

My sixteen men consisted, in the first instance, of Ensign Henderson, of the 56th Native Infantry, five or six of the Madras Fusileers, two platelayers from the railway works, and some men of the 84th Regiment. This first installment was soon disabled. The Madras Fusileers were armed with the Enfield rifle, and, consequently, they had to bear the brunt of the attack; they were all shot at their posts; several of the 84th also fell; but, in consequence of the importance of the position, as soon as a loss in my little corps was reported, Captain Moore sent me over a reinforcement from the intrenchment. Sometimes a civilian, sometimes a soldier came. The orders given us were not to surrender with our lives, and we did our best to obey them, though it was only by an amount of fatigue that in the retrospect now seems scarcely possible to have been a fact, and by the perpetration of such wholesale carnage that nothing could have justified in us but the instinct of self preservation, and I trust the equally strong determination to shelter the women and children to the latest moment. There was one advantage in the out picket station, in the fact that we were somewhat removed from the sickening spectacles continually occurring in the intrenchment. Sometimes, when relieved by a brother officer for a few moments, I have run across to the main guard for a chat with some old chums, or to join in the task of attempting to cheer the spirits of the women; but the sight there was always of a character to make me return to the barrack, relieved by the comparative quiet of its seclusion. We certainly had no diminished share of the conflict in the barracks, but we had not the heaps of wounded sufferers, nor the crowd of helpless ones whose agonies nothing could relieve.

The well in the intrenchment was one of the greatest points of danger, as the enemy invariably fired grape upon that spot as soon as any person made his appearance there to draw water. Even in the dead of night the darkness afforded but little protection, as they could hear the creaking of the tackle, and took the well known sound as a signal for instantly opening with their artillery upon the suttlers. These were chiefly privates, who were paid as much as eight or ten shillings per bucket. Poor fellows! their earnings were of little avail to them; but to their credit it must be said, that when money had lost its value, by reason of the extremity of our danger, they were not less willing to incur the risk of drawing for the women and the children. The constant riddling of shot soon tore away the wood and brickwork that surrounded the well, and the labor of drawing became much more prolonged and perilous. The water was between sixty and seventy feet from the surface of the ground, and with mere hand over hand labor it was wearisome work. My friend, John M'Killop, of the Civil Service, greatly distinguished himself here; he became self constituted captain of the well. He jocosely said that he was no fighting man, but would make himself useful where he could, and accordingly he took this post, drawing for the supply of the women and the children as often as he could. It was less than a week after he had undertaken this self denying service, when his numerous escapes were followed by a grape shot wound in the groin and speedy death. Disinterested even in death, his last words were an earnest entreaty that somebody would go and draw water for a lady to whom he had promised it. The sufferings of the women and children from thirst were intense, and the men could scarcely endure the cries for drink, which were almost perpetual from the poor little babes; terribly unconscious they were, most of them, of the great, great cost at which only it could be procured. I have seen the children of my brother officers sucking the pieces of old water bags, putting scraps of canvas and leather straps into the mouth to try and get a single drop of moisture upon their parched lips. Not even a pint of water was to be had for washing from the commencement to the close of the siege; and those only who have lived in India can imagine the calamity of such a privation to delicate women, who had been accustomed to the most frequent and copious ablutions as a necessary of existence. Had the relieving force, which we all thought to have been on its way from Calcutta, ever seen our beleaguered party, strange indeed would the appearance presented by any of us after the first week or ten days have seemed to them.

Tattered in clothing, begrimed with dirt, emaciated in countenance, were all without exception; faces that had been beautiful were now chiseled with deep furrows; haggard despair seated itself where there had been, a month before, only smiles. Some were sinking into the settled vacancy of look which marked insanity. The old, babbling with confirmed imbecility, and the young raving, in not a few cases, with wild mania; while only the strongest retained the calmness demanded by the occasion. And yet, looking back upon the horrible straits to which the women were driven, the maintenance of modesty and delicate feeling by them to the last, is one of the greatest marvels of the heart rending memories of those twenty one days.

Besides the well within the intrenchment, to which reference has been made, there was another close to barrack No. 3, upon which we looked, and to which we often repaired with sorrowing hearts. We drew no water there, it was our cemetery; and in three weeks we buried therein two hundred and fifty of our number.

When General Havelock recovered Cawnpore, he gave orders to fill up this vast grave, AND THE MOUND OF EARTH WHICH MARKS THAT MEMORABLE SPOT WAITS FOR THE MONUMENT WHICH WILL, I HOPE, BEFORE LONG RECORD THEIR SERVICES AND THEIR SUFFERINGS WHO SLEEP BENEATH. The burial of Sir John Moore, which has been taken to be the type of military funerals performed under fire, was elaborate in comparison with our task, who, with stealthy step, had under cover of the night to consign our lost ones in the most hurried manner to the deep, which at least secured their remains from depredation by carnivorous animals, and from the ignominious brutality of more savage men.

As soon as the siege had commenced, both of the barracks inside the intrenchment were set apart for the shelter of women and children, the worst cases of the invalids of the 32d Regiment, together with some of our superior officers. The majority of the male refugees who availed themselves of this shelter, were those who were thoroughly incapacitated by age or disease from enduring the toil and the heat of the trenches. I deeply regret, however, to have to record the fact that there was one officer of high rank, and in the prime of life, who never showed himself outside the walls of the barrack, nor took even the slightest part in the military operations. This craven hearted man, whose name I withhold out of consideration for the feelings of his surviving relatives, seemed not to possess a thought beyond that of preserving his own worthless life. Throughout three weeks of skulking, while women and children were daily dying around him, and the little band of combatants was being constantly thinned by wounds and death, not even the perils of his own wife could rouse this man to exertion; and when at length we had embarked at the close of the siege, while our little craft was stuck upon a sand bank, no expostulation could make him quit the shelter of her bulwarks, though we were adopting every possible expedient to lighten her burden. It was positively a relief to us when we found that his cowardice was unavailing; and a bullet through the boat's side that dispatched him caused the only death that we regarded with complacency.

One of the two barracks in the intrenched position was a strong building, and puckah roofed, that is, covered in with masonry. It had been originally the old dragoon hospital, and consisted of one long central room, surrounded by others of much smaller dimensions. After a day or two of the sharp cannonading to which we were exposed, all the doors, windows, and framework of this, the best of the two structures, were entirely shot away. Not a few of its occupants were killed by splinters, and a still greater number by the balls and bullets which flew continually through the open spaces, which were soon left without a panel or sash of wood to offer any resistance. Others died from falling bricks, and pieces of timber dislodged by shot. The second barrack had from the commencement excited serious apprehension lest its thatched roof should be set on fire. An imperfect attempt had been made to cover the thatch with tiles and bricks, and any materials at hand that would preserve the roof from conflagration. But after about a week the dreaded calamity came upon us. A carcass or shell filled with burning materials settled in the thatch, and speedily the whole barrack was in a blaze. As a part of this building had been used for a hospital, it was the object of the greatest solicitude to remove the poor fellows who lay there suffering from wounds and unable to move themselves. From one portion of the barrack the women and the children were running out, from another little parties laden with some heavy burden of suffering brotherhood were seeking the adjacent building. As this fire broke out in the evening, the light of the flames made us conspicuous marks for the guns of our brutal assailants, and without regard to sex or age, or the painful and protracted toil of getting out the sufferers, they did not cease till long after midnight to pour upon us incessant volleys of musketry. By means of indomitable perseverance many a poor agonizing private was rescued from the horrible death that seemed inevitable, but though all was done that ingenuity could suggest, or courage and determination accomplish, two artillerymen unhappily perished in the flames. The livid blaze of that burning barrack lighted up many a terrible picture of silent anguish, while the yells of the advancing Sepoys and the noise of their artillery filled the air with sounds that still echo in the ears of the only two survivors.

That was a night indeed to be long remembered. The enemy, imagining that all our attention was directed to the burning pile, took occasion to plan an assault. They advanced by hundreds under the shelter of the darkness, and without a sound from that side, with the intention of storming Ashe's battery, and they were allowed to come within sixty or eighty yards of the guns, before a piece was fired or a movement made to indicate that they were observed. Just when it must have appeared to them that their success was certain, our nine-pounders opened upon them with a most destructive charge of grape; the men shouldered successive guns which they had by their sides ready loaded; every available piece was discharged right into their midst, and in half an hour they left a hundred corpses in the open.

In the burnt barrack all our medical stores were consumed; not one of the surgical instruments was saved, and from that time the agonies of the wounded became most intense, and, from the utter impossibility of extracting bullets, or dressing mutilations, casualties were increased in their fatality. It was heartbreaking work to see the poor sufferers parched with thirst that could be only most scantily relieved, and sinking from fever and mortification that we had no appliances wherewith to resist.

After the destruction of the thatched barrack, as that which survived the fire would not accommodate the whole party, numbers of women and children were compelled to go out into the trenches, and not less than two hundred of them passed twelve days and nights upon the bare ground. Many of these were wives and daughters of officers, who had never known privation in its mildest form. Efforts were at first made to shelter them from the heat by erecting canvas stretchers overhead, but as often as the paltry covering was put up, it was fired by the enemy's shells. But our heroic sisters did not give all themselves up to despair even yet; they handed round the ammunition, encouraged the men to the utmost, and in their tender solicitude and unremitting attention to the wounded, though all smeared with powder and covered with dirt, they were more to be admired then than they had often been in far different costume, when arrayed for the glittering ballroom.

Mrs. White, a private's wife, was walking with her husband under cover, as they thought, of the wall, her twin children were one in each arm, when a single bullet passed through her husband; killing him, it passed also through both her arms, breaking them, and close beside the breathless husband and father fell the widow and her babes; one of the latter being also severely wounded. I saw her afterward in the main guard lying upon her back, with the two children, twins, laid one at each breast, while the mother's bosom refused not what her arms had no power to administer. Assuredly no imagination or invention ever devised such pictures as this most horrible siege was constantly presenting to our view.

Mrs. Williams, the widow of Colonel Williams, after losing her husband early in the siege, from apoplexy supervening upon a wound, was herself shot in the face; she lingered two days in frightful suffering and disfigurement, all the time attended by her intrepid daughter, who was herself suffering from a bullet wound right through the shoulder blade.

An ayah, while nursing the infant child of Lieutenant J. Harris, Bengal Engineers, lost both her legs by a round shot, and the little innocent was picked off the ground suffused in its nurse's blood, but completely free from injury. While we were at Cuttack the mother of this infant had died, and Captain and Mrs. Belson kindly undertook its charge; in what manner the poor little nursling's short but troubled life was terminated I know not.

Miss Brightman, the sister of Mrs. Harris, died of fever consequent upon the fatigue she had incurred in nursing Lieutenant Martin, who was wounded in the lungs. Martin was quite young; he only reached Cawnpore a day or two before the outbreak. He said to me one day soon after his arrival, "I should like to see some practice with these things," pointing to a heap of shells. He soon saw far more of that practice than most soldiers three times his age.

Mrs. Evans, the wife of Major Evans, Bombay Native Infantry, was killed by falling bricks, displaced by round shot.

My friend, Major Evans, had to endure the most intense solicitude for his beloved wife, while he was engaged in the defense of Lucknow.

Mrs. Reynolds, the wife of Captain Reynolds, 53d Native Infantry, was wounded in the wrist by a musket ball, and died of fever in consequence of there being no instruments or materials to alleviate her sufferings. Her husband had been previously killed by a round shot, which took off his arm. A Eurasian and her daughter, crouching behind an empty barrel, were both instantly killed by one shot.

The children were a constant source of solicitude to the intrenched party. Sometimes the little things, not old enough to have the instinct for liberty crushed by the presence of death, would run away from their mothers and play about under the barrack walls, and even on these the incarnate fiends would fire their muskets, and not a few were slain and wounded thus.

One poor woman, a private's wife, ran out from the cover of the barracks with a child in each hand, courting relief from her prolonged anguish by death from the Sepoy guns, but a private nobly went out and dragged them back to a sheltered position.

There were children born as well as dying in these terrible times, and three or four mothers had to undergo the sufferings of maternity in a crisis that left none of that hope and joy which compensate the hour of agony. One of the most painful of these cases was that of Mrs. Darby, the wife of a surgeon in the Company's service. Her husband had been ordered to Lucknow immediately before the mutiny, and was killed there. Mrs. Darby survived her accouchement, and was, I believe, one of those who perished in the boats.

Besides such constantly occurring and frightful spectacles as these, deaths from sunstroke and fever were frequently happening. Colonel Williams, 56th Native Infantry, Major Prout, Sir George Parker, and several of the privates died thus. The fatal symptoms were headache and drowsiness, followed by vomiting and gradual insensibility, which terminated in death. Privation, and the influence of the horrible sights which day after day presented, drove some to insanity, such was the case with one of the missionaries of the Society for the Propagation of the Gospel, the Rev. Mr. Haycock. He had been accustomed to bring out his aged mother every evening into the veranda, for a short relief from the fetid atmosphere within the barrack walls; the old lady was at length severely wounded, and her acute sufferings overcame the son's reason, and he died a raving maniac. There was also another clergyman connected with the Propagation Society in the intrenchment, the Rev. Mr. Cockey, though I am not aware of the manner in which he met his death. The station chaplain, the

Rev. Mr. Moncrieff, was most indefatigable in the performance of his ministry of mercy with the wounded and the dying. Public worship in any combined form was quite out of the question, but this devoted clergyman went from post to post reading prayers while we stood to arms. Short and interrupted as these services were, they proved an invaluable privilege, and there was a terrible reality about them, since in each such solemnity one or more of the little group gathered about the person of their instructor was sure to be present for the last time. Mr. Moncrieff was held in high estimation by the whole garrison before the mutiny, on account of the zealous manner in which he discharged the duties of his sacred office, but his self denial and constancy in the thickest of our perils made him yet more greatly beloved by us all. The Romish priest was the only well fed man in our party, for the Irish privates used to contribute from their scanty rations for his support: he died about the middle of the siege from sunstroke or apoplexy.

The frequency of our casualties from wounds may be best understood by the history of one short hour. Lieutenant Prole had come to the main guard to see Armstrong, the Adjutant of the 53d Native Infantry, who was unwell. While engaged in conversation with the invalid, Prole was struck by a musket ball in the thigh, and fell to the ground. I put his arm upon my shoulder, and holding him round the waist, endeavored to hobble across the open to the barrack, in order that he might obtain the attention of the surgeons there. While thus employed, a ball hit me under the right shoulder blade, and we fell to the ground together, and were picked up by some privates, who dragged us both back to the main guard. While I was lying on the ground, woefully sick from the wound, Gilbert Bax, 48th Native Infantry, came to condole with me, when a bullet pierced his shoulder blade, causing a wound from which he died before the termination of the siege.

Mr. Hillersden, the collecting magistrate of Cawnpore, and brother of Major Hillersden, who commanded the 53d Native Infantry, was standing in the veranda of the puckah roofed barrack in conversation with his wife, who had only recently recovered from her accouchement, when a round shot from the mess house of the 56th Native Infantry completely disemboweled him. His wife only survived him two or three days; she was killed by a number of falling bricks dislodged by a shot and causing concussion of the brain. Mrs. Hillersden was a most accomplished lady, and by reason of her cheerfulness, amiability, and piety, universally a favorite at the station.

In the same barrack Lieutenant G. R. Wheeler, son and aid-de-camp of the General, was sitting upon a sofa, fainting from a wound he had received in the trenches; his sister was fanning him, when a round shot entered the doorway, and left him a headless trunk; one sister at his feet, and father, mother, and another sister, in different parts of the same room, were witnesses of the appalling spectacle. Three officers, belonging to the same regiment with Lieutenant Wheeler, the 1st Native Infantry, namely, Lieutenants Smith and Redman, and Ensign Supple, had their heads taken off by round shots in the redan.

Lieutenant Dempster, who left a wife and four children, fell mortally wounded between Whiting's battery and the puckah roofed barrack.

Lieutenant Jervis, of the Engineers, fell in the same locality. He always scorned to run, and while calmly walking across the open, in the midst of a shower of bullets, some of us cried out to him, "Run, Jervis! Run!" but he refused, and was killed by a bullet through his heart.

Mr. Jack, brother of the Brigadier, who was on a visit from Australia, was hit by a round shot, which carried away his left leg. As this occurred before the destruction of the instruments, he underwent amputation, but sank under the operation.

Colonel Ewart, a brave and clever man, was severely wounded in the arm early in the proceedings, and was entirely disabled from any participation in the defense.

Captain Kempland suffered so much from the heat, that, although not wounded, he was also utterly prostrate and noncombatant. His European manservant made an attempt to get down the river with his master's baggage, but was taken by the Sepoys and murdered.

Lieutenant R. Quin died of fever. His brother, C. Quin, survived the siege, and was left severely wounded in the boat at Soorajpore.

Ensign Dowson suffered severely from sun stroke, and Ensign Foreman was wounded in the leg. Both of these youths perished at the boats.

Major Lindsay was struck in the face by the splinters caused by a round shot; he lay for a few days in total blindness and extreme pain, when death came to his relief. His disconsolate widow followed him a day or two afterward, slain by grief.

Mr. Heberden, of the railway service, was handing one of the ladies some water, when a charge of grape entered the barrack, and a shot passed through both his hips, leaving an awful wound. He lay for a whole week upon his face, and was carried upon a mattress down to the boats, where he died. The fortitude he had shown in active service did not forsake him during his extraordinary sufferings, for not a murmur escaped his lips.

Lieutenant Eckford, while sitting in the veranda, was struck by a round shot in the heart, causing instant death. He was an excellent artillery officer, and could ill be spared; besides his high military accomplishments this gentleman was an admirable linguist, and his death was a great loss to his country. To our enfeebled community these bereavements were a deplorable calamity.

Such are some specimens of the horrors endured, but by no means a summary of the long catalogue of lamentation and woe. Many casualties occurred of which I never heard, some probably which I have forgotten. Long and painful as this narrative of suffering may prove to the reader, he will not forget that all this was but on the surface; the agony of mind, the tortures of despair, the memories of home, the yearning after the distant children or parents, the secret prayers, and all the hidden heart wounds contained in those barracks, were, and must remain, known only to God.

It would be unjust to overlook the fact that a large number of the natives shared with us our sharp and bitter troubles. There were not a few native servants who remained in the intrenchment with their masters. Three of them, in the service of Lieutenant Bridges, were killed by one shell. One, belonging to Lieutenant Goad, 56th Native Infantry, was crossing to barrack No. 2, with some food in his hand, and was shot through the head. Several outlived the siege, and died at the time of embarkation; some two or three escaped after the capitulation, and from these persons the various and conflicting statements of our history have come piecemeal into the Indian and English newspapers.

Soon after the destruction of the hospital, it was determined upon by Captain Moore to make a dash upon the enemy's guns, in the hope of silencing some of these destructive weapons, and thus lessening the severity of the attack. Accordingly a party of fifty, headed by the Captain, sallied out at midnight, toward the church compound, where they spiked two or three guns. Proceeding thence to the mess house, they killed several of the native gunners, asleep at their posts, blew up one of the twenty-four-pounders, and spiked another or two; but although it was a most brilliant, daring, and successful exploit, it availed us little, as the next day they brought fresh guns into position, and this piece of service cost us one private killed and four wounded.

Day after day, throughout the whole period of our sufferings, while our numbers were more than decimated by the enemy's fire, and our supply of food was known to be running short, we were buoyed up by expectations of relief. General Wheeler had telegraphed for reinforcements before communication with Calcutta was broken off, and it was reported that the Governor-General had promised to send them up promptly, and we indulged the hope that they must have been expedited for our relief. We ministered all the comfort we could to the women, by the assurance that our desperate condition must be known at headquarters; but so effectually had the Sepoys closed the road all around us, that the tidings of our exact circumstances did not even reach Lucknow, only fifty miles distant, till the siege was nearly concluded. The southern road was entirely shut up, and not a native was allowed to travel in the direction of Allahabad. Pickets of Sepoy infantry were posted fifteen paces apart, so as to form a complete cordon around the position, and these were supported by cavalry pickets, forming a second circle, and the whole were relieved every two hours.

All the while that our numbers were rapidly diminishing, those of our antagonists were as constantly increasing. Revolters poured into the ranks from Delhi, Jhansi, Bangor, and Lucknow, and, at last, there were said to be not fewer than eight thousand of them in immediate proximity to us.

Often we imagined that we heard the sounds of distant cannonading. At all hours of the day and night my men have asked me to listen. Their faces would gladden with the delusive hope of a relieving force close at hand, but only to sink back again presently into the old care worn aspect. Weariness and want had alike to be forgotten, and the energy of desperation thrown into our unequal conflict. Occasionally moved by such rumors as these into a momentary gleaming of hope, the countenances of the women, for the most part, assumed a stolid apathy and a deadly stillness that nothing could move. Much excitement was caused in our midst, at the expiration of the first fortnight, by the arrival of a native spy, who came into the intrenchment in the garb of a bheestie, a water carrier. This man declared himself favorable to our cause, and said that he had brought good news, for there were two companies of European soldiers on the other side of the river, with a couple of guns from Lucknow; that they were making arrangements to cross the Ganges, and might be expected in our midst on the morrow. He came in again the next day, and told us that our countrymen were prevented crossing the stream by the rising of the waters, but that they were constructing rafts, and we might look for them in a day or two at the farthest. The tidings spread from man to man, and lighted some flickering rays of hope even in the bosoms of those who had abandoned themselves to despair. But days rolled on, and more terrific nights; and the delusion was dispelled like the mirage. Our pretended friend was, in fact, one of the Nana's spies, and the tidings which he conveyed back of our abject condition must have greatly gratified his sanguinary employer. I have no doubt that the fiction about approaching help was the invention of the wily

Azimoolah, and intended to throw us off our guard, and, by the relaxation of our vigilance, prepare the way for an assault. It had not that effect, though it was too successful in bolstering up our vain expectations. It will be remembered by my readers, that no relief reached Cawnpore till three weeks after the capitulation, when the invincible Havelock wrested the cantonments from the treacherous Nana. Would that his unparalleled feats of valor had met with the reward which, in his large heart, he so much coveted! the privilege of rescuing some of his countrywomen from the fangs of their brutal murderer. That was the guerdon for which he fought, and it was more cherished by him than all the honors of successful war; but an inscrutable Providence had otherwise ordained it.

The 28d of June, 1857, the centenary of the battle of Plassy, was, no doubt, intended to have been the date of a simultaneous preconcerted effort to break off the British yoke from the Himalayas to the Hoogly. Had not events at Meerut precipitated the outburst in its riper form, it must have proved exceedingly more successful than it actually became.

The Nana and his company evidently intended the celebration of this epoch after their own fashion. In the night of the 22d we were threatened in our barrack No. 2 by a storming party from barrack No. 1. We saw the pandies gathering to this position from all parts, and, fearing that my little band would be altogether overpowered by numbers, I sent to Captain Moore for more men. The answer was not altogether unexpected: "Not one could be spared." Shortly afterward, however, the gallant Captain came across to me, in company with Lieutenant Delafosse, and he said to me:

"Thompson, I think I shall try a new dodge; we are going out into the open, and I shall give the word of command as though our party were about to commence an attack."

Forthwith they sallied out; Moore with a sword, Delafosse with an empty musket.

The Captain vociferated to the winds, "Number one to the front." And hundreds of ammunition pouches rattled on the bayonet sheathe as our courageous foes vaulted out from the cover afforded by heaps of rubbish, and rushed into the safer quarters presented by the barrack walls. We followed them with a vigorous salute, and as they did not show fight just then, we had a hearty laugh at the ingenuity which had devised, and the courage which had executed, this successful feint. The whole of that night witnessed a series of surprises and false charges upon our barracks, and not a man of us left his post for an instant. Toward dawn, when they were a little more quiet, Mr. Mainwaring, a cavalry cadet, who was one of my picket, kindly begged of me to lie down a little while, and he would keep a sharp look out. It was indeed a little while, for I had scarcely closed my eyes when Mainwaring shouted, "Here they come." They advanced close up to the doorway of our barrack, which, in consequence of the floor not being down, presented brick work breast high, but had no door. They had never before shown so much pluck. Mainwaring's revolver dispatched two or three; Stirling, with an Enfield rifle, shot one and bayoneted another; both charges of my double barreled gun were emptied, and not in vain. We were seventeen of us inside that barrack, and they left eighteen corpses lying outside the doorway. An attack on the intrenchment was simultaneous with that on both of our barracks. They surrounded the walls on all sides, and in every style of uniform, regular and irregular, both cavalry and infantry, together with horse and bullock batteries of field artillery, sent out as skirmishers. Their cavalry started upon the charge from the riding school, and in their impetuosity, or through the ignorance of their leader, came all the way at a gallop, so that when they neared the intrenchment their horses were winded, and a round from our guns threw their ranks into hopeless confusion, and all who were not biting the dust, wheeled round and retired. They had started with the intention of killing us all, or dying in the attempt, and oaths had been administered to the principal men among them to insure their fidelity to that purpose, as well as to stimulate their courage and determination, but all the appliances employed were of none effect, so soon as one of our batteries lodged a charge of grape in their midst. One very singular expedient that they adopted upon this occasion to cover their skirmishers from our fire, was the following: they rolled before them great bales of cotton, and under the effectual security which it seemed to present from being struck by our shots, they managed to approach ominously near to our walls. The well directed fire from the batteries presently set light to some of these novel defenses, and panic struck the skirmishers retreated, before their main had shown signs of advance. During the following night we went out and brought in some of the cotton that had escaped the flames, and it was useful for stopping gaps made in the walls, and similar purposes. During the course of these manifestations I had a memento of the 23d of June, in the shape of a wound in the left thigh from a grapeshot, which plowed up the flesh, but happily, though narrowly, escaped the bone. On the evening of the 23d of June, a party of Sepoys came out unarmed, and having salaamed to us, obtained leave to take away the dead they had left outside our walls. There can be no doubt that the failure of the attack on this occasion was a grievous disappointment to the Nana and his coadjutors.

Seventeen days and nights our little party had resisted all the efforts made by the overwhelming numbers of the foe to storm the position. There remained nothing now for them to do but to starve us out; henceforth they abandoned all attempts to take us by assault. They resumed the whole work of annoyance, by coming every day up the lines and threatening us. Accordingly we had to resume the daily employment of expelling them, lest their unchecked insolence should lead to acts more decisive. After having made one of these charges through the whole tier of buildings, Captain Jenkins and I were returning from barrack to barrack to our pickets, surveying the effects of the sortie we had just concluded. We had sent on our men before us to resume their posts; and while we were leisurely walking and chatting together between the barracks numbered 4 and 5, a wounded Sepoy, who had feigned death while our men passed him, suddenly raised his musket and shot Captain Jenkins through the jaw. I had the miserable satisfaction of first dismissing the assailant, and then conducted my suffering companion to his barrack. He lived two or three days in excruciating agony, and then died from exhaustion, as it was quite impossible, without the aid of instruments, to get even the wretched nutriment we possessed into his throat. In Captain Jenkins we lost one of the bravest and one of the best of our party. Captain Moore took the post vacated by this sad event for the remainder of the siege.

On the 24th of June, a private named Blenman, a Eurasian by birth, but so dark in complexion as easily to have been taken for a native, and who had gone out once or twice before to the Nana's camp to report the state of affairs in that direction, was once more sent out with instructions, if possible, to reach Allahabad, and make known our desperate condition. He passed through my outpost disguised as a cook, with only a pistol and fifteen rupees in his possession. He managed to elude the observation of seven troopers who were posted as cavalry pickets, but he was discovered by the eighth, and when he endeavored to pass himself off as a chumar, or leather dresser, from the native city, whether they believed his story or not, they stripped him of rupees and pistol, and told him to return to the place he came from. Blenman was exceedingly courageous, and when he chose, one of the best men we had, but he was always fitful in temper, and at times difficult to manage. Two or three attempts of the same kind were made to open communications with the down country people, but they all failed; and, with the exception of Blenman, we never saw any of our spies again after they had quitted our walls. One of them, Mr. Shepherd, of the commissariat department, survives, and has published the account of his adventures, from which it appears that he volunteered his services to General Wheeler, in the hope of being able to provide a retreat for his family in the native city. He says:

"With this view I applied to the General, on the 24th of

June, for permission to go, at the same time offering to bring all the correct information that I might collect in the city, asking as a condition, that on my return, if I should wish it, my family might be allowed to leave the intrenchment. This, my request, was granted, as the General wished very much to get such information, and for which purpose he had previously sent out two or three natives at different times, under promises of high reward, but who never returned. He at the same time instructed me to try and negotiate with certain influential parties in the city, so as to bring about a rupture among the rebels, and cause them to leave off annoying us, authorizing me to offer a lac of rupees as a reward, with handsome pensions for life, to any person who would bring about such a thing. This, I have every reason to believe, could have been carried out successfully, had it pleased God to take me out unmolested; but it was not so ordained, it was merely a means, under God's providence, to save me from sharing the fate of the rest, for as I came out of the intrenchment, disguised as a native cook, and passing through the new unfinished barracks, had not gone very far when I was taken a prisoner, and under custody of four Sepoys and a couple of sowers, all well armed, was escorted to the camp of the Nana, and was ordered to be placed under a guard. Here several questions were put to me concerning our intrenchment, not by the Nana himself, but by some of his people, to all of which I replied as I was previously instructed by our General; for I had taken the precaution of asking him what I should say in case I was taken. My answers were not considered satisfactory, and I was confronted with two women servants, who three days previously had been caught in making their escape from the intrenchment, and who gave a version of their own, making it appear that the English were starving, and not able to hold out much longer, as their number was greatly reduced. I, however, stood firm to what I had first mentioned, and they did not know which party to believe. I was kept under custody till the 12th of July, on which date my trial took place, and I was sentenced to three years' imprisonment, with hard labor. They gave me only parched grain to eat daily, and that in small quantities."

The arrival of General Havelock was the means of Mr. Shepherd's release after twenty five days' captivity. In this gentleman's generally truthful narrative of the siege, there is one misstatement which requires correction, as it may have caused in some quarters the belief that we could have held out a fortnight longer than we did. Mr. Shepherd says that on the 24th June "there were provisions yet left to keep the people alive on half rations for the next fifteen or twenty days." This is an error, as when the capitulation was projected, we had already been placed several days on half rations, and there were then in stock only supplies sufficient for four more days at the reduced rate.

Many attempts were made to introduce themselves into our midst as spies by emissaries of the Nana, but with the exception of the man who brought us the story of the approaching relief, they failed as conspicuously as our own efforts in that direction. The natives are exceedingly adroit in this kind of occupation; they secrete their brief dispatches in quills most mysteriously concealed about the person; they keep ambush with the most patient self possession, and creep through the jungles as stealthily as the jackal. Often when our sentries were on the lookout over the wall, they have detected Sepoys creeping on all fours with their tulwars between the teeth in the attempt to cut down a man without observation, but fortunately none of our force were caught napping in that way.

THE CAPITULATION.

On the twenty first day of the siege, the firing of my picket having ceased for a short time, the lookout man up in the crow's nest shouted, "There 's a woman coming across." She was supposed to have been a spy, and one of the picket would have shot her, but that I knocked down his arm and saved her life. She had a child at her breast, but was so imperfectly clothed as to be without shoes and stockings. I lifted her over the barricade in a fainting condition, when I recognized her as Mrs. Greenway, a member of a wealthy family who had resided at Cawnpore, and carried on their operations as merchants in the cantonments. Upon the appearance of the mutiny they fled to Nuzzuffghur, where they had a factory, in the belief that their own villagers would be quite able to protect them from any serious injury. These precautions were, however, utterly useless, as they fell into the Nana's hands.

One of the members of this family paid the Nana three lacs of rupees, £30,000, to save the lives of the entire household. The unprincipled monster took the ransom, but numbered all the Greenways among the slain. As soon as she had recovered herself after entering the barrack, Mrs. Greenway handed me a letter with this superscription:

"TO THE SUBJECTS OF HER MOST GRACIOUS
MAJESTY, QUEEN VICTORIA."

I took this document to Captain Moore, and he, together
with General Wheeler and Captain Whiting, deliberated over its
contents, they were as follows:

"All those who are in no way connected with the acts of
Lord Dalhousie, and are willing to lay down their arms, shall
receive a safe passage to Allahabad."

There was no signature to it, but the handwriting was
that of Azimoolah. Sir Hugh Wheeler, still hopeful of relief
from Calcutta, and suspicious of treachery on the part of the
Nana, for a long time most strenuously opposed the idea of
making terms; but upon the representation that there were only
three days' rations in store, and after the often reiterated claims
of the women and children, and the most deplorable destitution
in which we were placed, he at last succumbed to Captain
Moore's expostulations, and consented to the preparation of a
treaty of capitulation. All of us who were juniors adopted the
views of the brave old General, but we well knew that it was
only consideration for the weak and the wounded, that turned
the vote against us. Had there been only men there, I am sure
we should have made a dash for Allahabad rather than have
thought of surrender; and Captain Moore would have been the
first to lead the forlorn hope. A braver soul than he never

breathed.

It is easy enough, in the comfortable retirement of the club dining room, for Colonel Pipeclay to call in question the propriety of the surrender; and his cousin, Mr. Scribe, in glowing trisyllabics, can fluently enough discourse of military honor and British heroism of olden times. Only let these gentlemen take into consideration in their wine and walnut arguments, the famished sucklings, the woe worn women, who awaited the issue of those deliberations, and perhaps even they will admit, as all true soldiers and sensible citizens have done, that there remained nothing better for our leaders to do than to hope the best from an honorable capitulation.

The whole of that 26th of June the enemy ceased firing upon us. While the deliberations were going on Mrs. Greenway staid in my picket, though all the time eager to return to her little children, whom her brutal captor had retained as hostages. She was interrogated particularly as to the treatment she had received, and gave distressing details of their cruelty. They had fed her only on a most starving allowance of chupatties and water; stripped her of all her clothing but a gown, and had pulled her earrings out through the flesh. She cried most bitterly while enumerating her wrongs, though she most explicitly affirmed that no indignities or abuse had molested her honor. She returned at night to the Nana's camp, bearing the message, that the General, Sir Hugh Wheeler, was in deliberation as to the answer that should be sent. Soon after Mrs. Greenway had left, Captain Moore reached my picket with the intelligence that we were about to treat with the enemy. I passed the word to the native officer stationed nearest to us, and presently Azimoolah made his appearance: he was accompanied by Juwallah Pershaud, the brigadier of the Nana's cavalry. These two came to within about two hundred yards of my barrack, and Captains Moore and Whiting, and Mr. Roche, postmaster of Cawnpore, went out to arrange the terms of the capitulation. The conditions for which our representatives stipulated, were honorable surrender of our shattered barracks and free exit under arms, with sixty rounds of ammunition per man; carriages to be provided for the conveyance of the wounded, the women and the children; boats furnished with flour to be ready at the ghaut. Some of the native party added to the remark about supplying us with flour, "We will give you sheep and goats also."

Azimoolah engaged to take these written proposals to the Nana, and the same afternoon they were sent back by a sowar, with the verbal message that the Nana agreed to all the conditions, and that the cantonments were to be evacuated the same night. This was utterly impossible, and the treaty was immediately returned with an intimation that our departure must be delayed till the morrow. The sowar came back to us once more, and Captain Whiting and I went out to meet him, when he informed us that the Nana was inflexible in his determination that we should instantly evacuate, and that if we hesitated his guns would open upon us again; and moreover he bade us remember that he was thoroughly acquainted with our impoverished condition; he knew that our guns were shattered, and if he did renew the bombardment, we must all certainly be killed. To all this Whiting replied we should never be afraid of their entering the intrenchment, as we had repelled their repeated attempts to do this, and even if they should succeed in overpowering us, we had men always ready at the magazines to blow us all up together. The sowar returned to the Nana, and by and by he came out to us again, with the verbal consent that we should delay the embarkation till the morning. Mr. Todd now volunteered to take the document across to the Sevadah Kothi, the Nana's residence, and after about an absence of half an hour, he returned with the treaty of capitulation signed by the Nana. Mr. Todd said that he was courteously received, and that no hesitation was made in giving the signature, which, in point of fact, left the covenant as worthless as it possibly could be. I narrate all these details, to exonerate General Wheeler and Captain Moore from any suspicion of having overlooked precautions that might be supposed to give security to their proceedings. Three men were sent from the hostile camp into our intrenchment to remain there the whole night as hostages for the Nana's good faith. One of them was the before named Juwallah Pershaud; there is little doubt that this rogue was in possession of a perfect programme of the projected plans for the morrow. He was one of the Bithoor retainers, and had now become a very considerable personage, having floated on the tide of mutiny to high military command in the ranks of the rebel army. Juwallah condoled in most eloquent language with Sir Hugh Wheeler upon the privations he had undergone, and said that it was a sad affair at his time of life for the General to suffer so much; and that after he had commanded Sepoy regiments for so many years, it was a shocking thing they should turn their arms against him. He, Juwallah, would take care that no harm should come to any of us on the morrow; and his companions used language of the same kind both for its obsequiousness and falsity. Before sunset our shattered guns were formally made over to the Nana, and a company of his artillery stood at them the whole night: some of them men who had been drilled at the same guns in the service of the Honorable East India Company. A committee was next appointed, consisting of Captain Athill Turner and Lieutenants Delafosse and Goad, to go down to the river and see if the boats were in readiness for our reception. An escort of native cavalry was sent to conduct them to the ghaut. They found about forty boats moored and apparently ready for departure, some of them roofed, and others undergoing that process. These were the large upcountry boats, so well known to all Indians. The committee saw also the apparent victualing of some of the boats, as in their presence a show of furnishing them with supplies was made, though before the morning there was not left in any of them a sufficient meal for a rat. Our delegates returned to us without the slightest molestation, though I afterward gathered that Captain Turner was made very uneasy by the repetition of the word *kuttle,* massacre, which he overheard passing from man to man by some of the 56th Native Infantry, who were present on the bank of the river.

During the night some sleepy sentry of theirs, in barrack No. 1, dropped his musket, and so caused its discharge. I suppose that at their headquarters this was taken to be firing on our part, for they instantly opened with musketry and artillery all around us, as rapidly as they could load repeating the volley. We did not answer them with a single cartridge, but stood at our posts prepared for an attack. Juwallah sent for one of the Sepoys in barrack No. 1; and upon discovering the cause of the commotion, dispatched a quieting communication to his uneasy principals. Notwithstanding this interruption, that night was by far the best we had had for a month. With a pillow of brickbats, made comfortable by extreme fatigue and prolonged suspense, and with a comfortable sense of having done all that he could, or that his country could require, many a poor fellow slept that night, only less soundly than he did on the following one. The well had been besieged on the cessation of the enemy's fire, and draught after draught was swallowed; and though the debris of mortar and bricks had made the water cloudy, it was more delicious than nectar. It was not given out by thimblefuls that night. Double rations of chupatties and dhal were served around, though the degree of confidence that was put in each other by the contracting parties will be tolerably evident from the fact that no decent food was begged or bought on our side, nor was it offered or given on the other. There was a slightly visible change for the better in the countenances of the women, though some of them gave expression to their suspicions with such inquiries as these, "Do you think it will be all right tomorrow?" "Will they really let us go down to Allahabad in safety?" The majority assumed a tone of cheerfulness, and comforted one another with the prospects of rescue. Such, however, was the extreme depression of both mind and body, that any alternative seemed preferable to the prolonged murder of the siege. The children, at least, were cheerful; they had had the wants of the moment more liberally supplied than for a long time past, and at midnight all was silent; men, women, and children, all slept. After such an acclimation of the brain to incessant bombardment, the stillness was actually painful. In that silence the angel of death brooded over many a sleeper there. The jackal took the opportunity offered to him to prowl among the animal remains around the intrenchment, without alarm from the guns; and daybreak disclosed to view hosts of adjutant birds and vultures gloating over their carnivorous breakfast. These are the only parties who have any cause to thank the Sepoys for the rebellion of 1857.

THE DEPARTURE.

It was a truly strange spectacle which the opening morning of the 27th of June brought within the intrenchment. All the activities of departure were manifest on every side. Men and women were loading themselves with what each thought most precious. Hurried words of sympathy were uttered to the wounded, and many a hearty declaration given that, at all hazards, they should not be left behind. Some had much that they wished to carry away, some had nothing. The time for deliberation was short, and the power to carry limited indeed. Little relics of jewelry were secreted by some, in the tattered fragments of their dress. A few were busily occupied in digging up boxes from the ruins of the building, the said boxes containing plate and other valuables. Some cherished a Bible or a prayer book; others bestowed all their care upon the heirlooms which the dead had intrusted to their keeping, to be transferred to survivors at home. The able bodied men packed themselves with all the ammunition which they could carry, till they were walking magazines.

Not a few looked down that well, and thought of the treasures consigned to its keeping. Some would have fain been among them even there. Here a party paced the outside of the barrack wall, and gazed at the brick work, all honeycombed with shot. There a little group lent kindly aid to bind up and secure the clothing that could scarcely be made to hold together. Never, surely, was there such an emaciated, ghostly party of human beings as we. There were women who had been beautiful, now stripped of every personal charm, some with, some without gowns; fragments of finery were made available no longer for decoration, but decorum; officers in tarnished uniforms, rent and wretched, and with nondescript mixtures of apparel, more or less insufficient in all. There were few shoes, fewer stockings, and scarcely any shirts; these had all gone for bandages to the wounded. After an hour or two of this busy traffic, the elephants and palanquins made their appearance at Ashe's battery. Water was the only cordial we could give to the wounded, but this they eagerly and copiously drank. No rations were served out before starting, nor was any ceremony or religious service of any kind observed. Sixteen elephants and between seventy and eighty palanquins composed the van of the mournful procession, and more than two hundred sufferers had thus to be conveyed down to the river. The advance guard, consisting of some men of the 32d Regiment, led by Captain Moore, had to return for a second installment of those who were unable to walk the single mile to the ghaut. Not a Sepoy accompanied us; we loaded and unloaded the burdens ourselves; and the most cautious handling caused much agony to our disabled ones. They would have been objects for intense pity, and subjects of great pain, with all the relief that hospital science could have devised for their attention, but our rude and unaided efforts must have caused them greatly aggravated torture.

The women and children were put on the elephants and into the bullock carts; the able bodied walked down indiscriminately after the advance had gone. Immediately after the exit of the first detachment the place was thronged with Sepoys. One of them said to one of our men, "Give me that musket!" placing his hand upon the weapon, as if about to take it. "You shall have its contents, if you please, but not the gun," was the reply; the proposal not having been accepted, the insulted Briton walked off: it was the only semblance of an interruption to our departure.

The Sepoys were loud in their expression of astonishment that we had withstood them so long, and said that it was utterly unaccountable to them. We told them that had it not been for the failure of our food, we should have held the place to the last man. I asked one of them, whom I recognized as having belonged to my own regiment, how many they had lost, and he told me from eight hundred to a thousand. I believe this estimate to have been under rather than over the mark.

Inquiries were made by men after their old officers whom they had missed, and they appeared much distressed at hearing of their death. Such discrepancies of character will, possibly, mystify the northern mind, but they are indigenous to the east. I inquired of another Sepoy of the 53d, "Are we to go to Allahabad without molestation?" He affirmed that such was his firm belief; and I do not suppose that the contemplated massacre had been divulged beyond the councils of its brutal projectors. Poor old Sir Hugh Wheeler, his lady and daughter, walked down to the boats. The rear was brought up by Major Vibart, who was the last officer in the intrenchment. Some of the rebels, who had served in this officer's regiment, insisted on carrying out the property which belonged to him. They loaded a bullock cart with boxes, and escorted the Major's wife and family down to the boats with the most profuse demonstrations of respect. When we reached the place of embarkation, all of us, men and women, as well as the bearers of the wounded and children, had to wade knee deep through the water to get into the boats, as not a single plank was provided to serve for a gangway. It was 9 o'clock, A. M., when the last boat received her complement. And now I have to attempt to portray one of the most brutal massacres that the history of the human race has recorded, aggravated, as it was, by the most reckless cruelty and monstrous cowardice.

The boats were about thirty feet long and twelve feet across the thwarts, and overcrowded with their freight. They were flat down on the sand banks, with about two feet of water rippling around them. We might and ought to have demanded an embarkation in deeper water, but, in the hurry of our departure, this had been overlooked. If the rainy season had come on while we were intrenched, our mud walls would have been entirely washed away, and grievous epidemic sickness must have been added to the long catalogue of our calamities. While the siege lasted we were daily dreading the approach of the rains, now, alas we mourned their absence; for the Ganges was at its lowest. Captain Moore had told us that no attempt at anything like order of progress would be made in the departure; but when all were aboard, we were to push off as quickly as possible, and make for the other aide of the river, where orders would be given for our further direction. As soon as Major Vibart had stepped into his boat, " Off!" was the word; but at a signal from the shore, the native boatmen, who numbered eight and a coxswain to each boat, all jumped over and waded to the shore. We fired into them immediately, but the majority of them escaped, and are now plying their old trade in the neighborhood of Cawnpore. Before they quitted us, these men had contrived to secrete burning charcoal in the thatch of most of the boats. Simultaneously with the departure of the boatmen, the identical troopers who had escorted Major Vibart to the ghaut opened upon us with their carbines. As well as the confusion, caused by the burning of the boats, would allow, we returned the fire of these horsemen, who were about fifteen or sixteen in number, but they retired immediately after the volley they had given us.,

Those of us who were not disabled by wounds now jumped out of the boats, and endeavored to push them afloat, but, alas most of them were utterly immovable. Now, from ambush, in which they were concealed all along the banks, it seemed that thousands of men fired upon us; besides four nine-pounders, carefully masked and pointed to the boats, every bush was filled with Sepoys.

There are two or three houses close down by the river in this place, one of them formerly known as the Fusileer mess house, the second the residence of Captain Jenkins, and a third now in the occupancy of the station chaplain. These were filled with our murderers, and the last of them held two of the guns. The scene which followed this manifestation of the infernal treachery of our assassins is one that beggars all description. Some of the boats presented a broadside to the guns, others were raked from stem to stern by the shot. Volumes of smoke from the thatch somewhat vailed the full extent of the horrors of that morning. All who could move were speedily expelled from the boats by the heat of the flames Alas! the wounded were burnt to death; one mitigation only there was to their horrible fate, the flames were terrifically fierce, and their intense sufferings were not protracted. Wretched multitudes of women and children crouched behind the boats, or waded out into deep water and stood up to their chins in the river to lessen the probability of being shot. Meanwhile Major Vibart's boat, being of lighter draught than some, had got off and was drifting down the stream, her thatched roof unburnt. I threw into the Ganges my father's Chuznee medal, and my mother's portrait, all the property I had left, determined they should only have my life for a prey; and with one final shudder at the deviltry enacting upon that bank, and which it was impossible to mitigate by remaining any longer in its reach, I struck out, swimming for the retreating boat. There were a dozen of us beating the water for life; close by my side there were two brothers, Ensign Henderson, 56th Native Infantry, and his brother, who had but recently come out to India. They both swam well for some distance, when the younger became weak, and although we encouraged him to the utmost, he went down in our sight, though not within our reach; presently his survivor, J. W. Henderson, was struck on the hand by a grape shot. He put the disabled arm over my shoulder, and with one arm each, we swam to the boat, which by this time had stranded on a bank close to the Oude side of the river. We were terribly exhausted when Captain Whiting pulled us in; and had it not been for the sand bank, we must have perished. All of the other swimmers sank through exhaustion, or were shot in the water, except Lieutenant Harrison, of the 2d Light Cavalry, and private Murphy, 84th regiment. Harrison had left one of the boats in company with a number of passengers, and by wading they reached a small island, about two hundred yards from the shore. While I was swimming past this islet, I saw three sowars of cavalry who had also waded from the Cawnpore bank. One of them cut down one of our women with his tulwar, and then made off for Harrison, who received him with a charge from his revolver, and waited for the second man, whom he dispatched in like manner, whereupon the third took to the water on the shore side of the ait, and Harrison, plunging in on the riverside, swam to Vibart's boat. While I was swimming, a second boat got away from the ghaut, and while drifting, was struck by a round shot below the water mark, and was rapidly filling, when she came along side, and we took off the survivors of her party. Now the crowded state of our poor ark left little room for working her. Her rudder was shot away; we had no oars, for these had all been thrown overboard by the traitorous boatmen, and the only implements that could be brought into use, were a spar or two, and such pieces of wood as we could in safety tear away from the sides. Grape and round shot flew about us from either bank of the river, and shells burst constantly on the sand banks in our neighborhood. Alternately stranding and drifting, we were often within a hundred yards of the guns on the Oude side of the river, and saw them load, prime, and fire into our midst. Shortly after midday we got out of range of their great guns; the sandy bed on the river bank had disabled their artillery bullocks, but they chased us the whole day, firing in volleys of musketry incessantly.

On the 27th of June we lost, after the escape of the boat, Captain Moore, Lieutenants Ashe, Bolton, Burney, and Glanville, besides many others, whose names I did not know. Captain Moore was killed while attempting to push off the boat, a ball pierced him in the region of the heart; Ashe and Bolton died in the same manner. Burney and Glanville were carried off by one round shot, which also shattered Lieutenant Fagan's leg to such an extent, that from the knee downward it was only held together by sinews. His sufferings were frightful, but he behaved with wonderful patience. I had a great regard for him, as he and I were griffs together at Benares. Just after I had been pulled into the boat, Mrs. Swinton, who was a relative of Lieutenant Jervis, of the Engineers, was standing up in the stern, and, having been struck by a round shot, fell overboard and sank immediately. Her poor little boy, six years old, came up to me and said, "Mamma has fallen overboard." I endeavored to comfort him, and told him mamma would not suffer any more pain. The little babe cried out, "O, why are they firing upon us? did not they promise to leave off?" I never saw the child after that, and suspect that he soon shared his mother's death.

The horrors of the lingering hours of that day seemed as if they would never cease; we had no food in the boat, and had nothing before starting. The water of the Ganges was all that passed our lips, save prayers, and shrieks, and groans

The wounded and the dead were often entangled together in the bottom of the boat: to extricate the corpses was a work of extreme difficulty, though imperatively necessary from the dreaded consequences of the intense heat, and the importance of lightening the boat as much as possible.

In the afternoon of that day I saw a Sepoy from behind a tree deliberately taking aim at me: the bullet struck the side of my head, and I fell into the boat stunned by the wound. "We were just going to throw you overboard," was the greeting I had from some of the men when I revived. Six miles was the entire distance that we accomplished in the whole day; at 5 P. M., we stranded, and as all our efforts to move the keel an inch were in vain, we resolved to stay there at all hazards till nightfall, in the hope that when darkness sheltered us we might be able to get out the women and lighten the craft sufficiently to push her off. They now sent a burning boat down the stream, in the hope that she would fall foul of us, providentially the thing glided past us, though within a yard or two.

At night they let fly arrows with lighted charcoal fastened to them, to ignite, if possible, the thatched roof, and this protection we were, in consequence, obliged to dislodge and throw overboard. When we did succeed in getting adrift, the work of pushing away from the sand banks was incessant; and we spent as much of the night out, as we did in the boat. There was no moon, however, and although they did not cease firing at us till after midnight, they did us little damage.

When the morning broke upon us, we saw none of our pursuers, and began to indulge the hope that they had given up the chase. We had, however, only made four miles in the entire night, and our prospects of escape can scarcely be said to have improved. About 8 A. M. we saw some natives bathing, and persuaded a native drummer, who was with us, to go and talk with them, and try to induce them to get us some food. The drummer took with him five rupees, and procured from one of the bathers a promise to obtain food, and also, if possible, the assistance of some native boatmen. This man left his *lotah*, a cooking pot, which the natives carry everywhere with them, as a guarantee for his fidelity; but we saw no more of him, and he informed our messenger that orders had been sent down to Nuzzuffghur, two miles further, to seize us, and that Baboo Ram Buksh of Dhownriakera, a powerful zemindar on the Oude side, had engaged that he would not suffer one of us to escape his territory. Captain Whiting now wrote with his pencil a brief statement of our utter abandonment of all hope, put the scrap of paper into a bottle, and cast it into the river. At 2 P. M. we stranded off Nuzzuffghur, and they opened on us with musketry. Major Vibart had been shot through one arm on the previous day; nevertheless he got out, and while helping to push off the boat was shot through the other arm. Captain Athill Turner had both his legs smashed. Captain Whiting was killed. Lieutenant Quin was shot through the arm; Captain Seppings through the arm; and Mrs. Seppings through the thigh. Lieutenant Harrison was shot dead. I took off his rings and gave them to Mrs. Seppings, as I thought the women might perhaps excite some commiseration, and that if any of our party escaped, it would be some of them. Blenman, our bold spy, was shot here in the groin, and implored some of us to terminate his sufferings with a bullet, but it might not be done. At this place they brought out a gun; but while they were pointing it at us the rain came down in such torrents that they were not able to discharge it more than once. At sunset fifty or sixty natives came down the stream in a boat from Cawnpore, thoroughly armed, and deputed to board and destroy us. But they also grounded on a sand bank; and instead of waiting for them to attack us, eighteen or twenty of us charged them, and few of their number escaped to tell the story. Their boat was well supplied with ammunition, and we appropriated it to our own use; but there was no food, and death was now staring us in the face from that direction. That night we fell asleep, faint and weary, and expecting never to see the morrow; but a hurricane came on in the night, and set us free again. Some of us woke in the mid darkness, and found the boat floating; some fresh hopes buoyed us up again; but daylight returned to reveal the painful fact that we had drifted out of the navigable channel into a siding of the river opposite Soorajpore. Our pursuers speedily discovered us, and again opened with musketry on the boat, which was once more settled down deep in a sandbank.

At 9 o'clock, A. M., Major Vibart directed me, with Lieutenant Delafosse, Sergeant Grady, and eleven privates of the 134th and 32d Regiments, to wade to the shore and drive off the Sepoys, while they attempted to ease off the boat again. It was a forlorn enterprise, that consigned to us, but it mysteriously contributed, by God's goodness, to the escape of four of our number. Maddened by desperation, we charged the crowd of Sepoys and drove them back some distance, till we were thoroughly surrounded by a mingled party of natives, armed and unarmed. We cut our way through these, bearing more wounds, but without the loss of a man; and reached the spot at which we had landed, but the boat was gone. Our first thought was that they had got loose again, and were farther down the stream; and we followed in that direction, but never saw either the boat or our doomed companions any more.

Our only hope of safety now was in flight; and, with a burning sun overhead, a rugged raviny ground, and no covering for the feet, it was no easy task for our half famished party to make head; but a rabble of ryots and Sepoys at our heels soon put all deliberation upon the course to be pursued, as it did ourselves, to flight. For about three miles we retreated, when I saw a temple in the distance, and gave orders to make for that. To render us less conspicuous as marks for the guns, we had separated to the distance of about twenty paces apart; from time to time loading and firing as we best could upon the multitude in our rear. As he was entering the temple, Sergeant Grady was shot through the head. I instantly set four of the men crouching down in the doorway with bayonets fixed, and their muskets so placed as to form a *cheval-de-frise* in the narrow entrance. The mob came on helter skelter in such maddening haste that some of them fell or were pushed on to the bayonets, and their transfixed bodies made the barrier impassable to the rest, upon whom we, from behind our novel defense, poured shot upon shot into the crowd. The situation was the more favorable to us, in consequence of the temple having been built upon a base of brick-work three feet from the ground, and approached by steps on one side. The brother of Baboo Ram Buksh, who was leading the mob, was slain here; and his bereaved relation was pleased to send word to the Nana that the English were thoroughly invincible. Foiled in their attempts to enter our asylum, they next began to dig at its foundation; but the walls had been well laid, and were not so easily to be moved as they expected. They now fetched fagots, and from the circular construction of the building they were able to place them right in front of the doorway with impunity, there being no window or loop hole in the place through which we could attack them, nor any means of so doing, without exposing ourselves to the whole mob at the entrance. In the center of the temple there was an altar for the presentation of gifts to the presiding deity; his shrine, however, had not lately been enriched, or it had more recently been visited by his ministering priests, for there were no gifts upon it. There was, however, in a deep hole in the center of the stone which constituted the altar, a hollow with a pint or two of water in it, which, although long since putrid, we bailed out with our hands, and sucked down with great avidity. When the pile of fagots had reached the top of the doorway, or nearly so, they set them on fire, expecting to suffocate us; but a strong breeze kindly sent the great body of the smoke away from the interior of the temple. Fearing that the suffocating, sultry atmosphere would be soon insupportable, I proposed to the men to sell their lives as dearly as possible; but we stood till the wood had sunk down into a pile of embers, and we began to hope that we might brave out their torture till night, apparently the only friend left us, would let us get out for food and attempted escape. But their next expedient compelled an evacuation for they brought bags of gunpowder, and threw them upon the red hot ashes. Delay would have been certain suffocation, so out we rushed. The burning wood terribly marred our bare feet, but it was no time to think of trifles. Jumping the parapet, we were in the thick of the rabble in an instant; we fired a volley, and ran a-muck with the bayonet. Seven of our number succeeded in reaching the bank of the river, and we first threw in our guns and then ourselves. The weight of ammunition we had in the pouches carried us under the water; while we were thus submerged, we escaped the first volley that they fired. We slipped off the belts, rose again, and swam; and by the time they had loaded a second time, there were only heads for them to aim at. I turned around, and saw the banks of the river thronged with the black multitude, yelling, howling, and firing at us; while others of their party rifled the bodies of the six poor fellows we had left behind. Presently two more were shot in the head; and one private, Ryan, almost sinking from exhaustion, swam into a sand bank and was knocked on the head by two or three ruffians waiting to receive him. These villains had first promised Lieutenant Delafosse and private Murphy that if they would come to the shore they should be protected, and have food given to them. They were so much inclined to yield that they made toward the bank, but suddenly and wisely altered their determination. Infuriated with disappointment, one of them threw his club at Delafosse; but in the hight of his energy lost his balance and fell into deep water; the other aimed at Murphy, and struck him on the heel. For two or three hours we continued swimming; often changing our position, and the current helping our progress. At length our pursuers gave up the chase; a sowar on horseback was the last we saw of them.

It turned out that we had reached the territory of a rajah who was faithful to Government, Dirigbijah Singh, of Moorar Mhow, in Oude. When no longer pursued, we turned into the shore to get rest, and saw two or three long nosed alligators basking on a sand bank. The natives afterward said that it was a miracle we had escaped their bottle nosed brethren who feed on men.

We were sitting down by the shore, with the water up to

our necks, still doubtful of our safety, when we heard voices and approaching footsteps, and again plunged into the stream, like terrified beasts of the waters. Our visitors proved to be retainers of the Rajah Dirigbijah Singh, though their armed aspect, with swords, shields, and matchlocks, and our ignorance of the loyal sanctions under which they lived, made them any thing but comforting in appearance to us. "Sahib! Sahib why swim away? we are friends!" they shouted. I replied to them, "We have been deceived so often, that we are not inclined to trust any body." They said if we wished it, they would throw their arms into the river to convince us of their sincerity. Partly from the exhaustion which was now beginning to be utterly insupportable, and partly from the hope that they were faithful, we swam to the shore, and when we reached the shallow water, such was our complete prostration that they were obliged to drag us out; we could not walk, our feet were burnt, and our frames famished. We had been swimming, without a moment's intermission, a distance of six miles since we left Soorajpore. They extricated me first; and having laid me down upon the bank, covered me with one of their blankets. The others shortly followed, and, being equally done up, were indulged, for a few minutes, in like manner. I had on me no clothing but a flannel shirt. My, coat and trowsers, such as they were, had been taken off in the river to facilitate progress. That flannel shirt I very greatly respect; it went into the siege a bright pink, just as it had come from the hands of Messrs. Thresher and Glenny, who delight in such gayeties; but if these very respectable venders could see it now they would never accredit it as from their establishment. Lieutenant Delafosse had nothing in the shape of clothing but a piece of sheeting round his loins; and his shoulders were so burnt by exposure to the sun, that the skin was raised in huge blisters, as if he had just escaped death by burning. Sullivan and Murphy were altogether destitute of clothing of any kind, said consequently suffered equally from the sun. Murphy had a cap pouch, full of rupees, tied round his right knee; but our generous preservers were not proof against the temptation, so they eased him of this load, and also of a ring which he wore, but when they found that this was made of English gold, which, on account of its alloy, the natives greatly despise, they gave it him back again.

After we had rested a little, our captors proposed that we should go to the adjacent village; and supported by a native on each side of us, with his hands under our arm pits, we partly walked, and were partly carried a distance that seemed to us many miles, though not, in reality, more than three or four furlongs. We were so enfeebled that, in crossing a little current which had to be waded, they were obliged to use great strength to prevent our being washed away. As soon as we reached the village, they took us to the hut of the zemindar, who received us most kindly, commiserated with us upon our horrible condition, and gave us a hearty meal of dhal, chupatties, and preserves.

THE ESCAPE.

It was the evening of the 29th of June when we reached Moorar Mhow, and since the night of the 26th we had not tasted solid food. We soon asked for soma information about the missing boat, and if it had passed down the river. They told us that it had been seized by a party of the Nana's men, and carried back to Cawnpore. While we were taking our food, a great crowd of the villagers surrounded the hut, and gazed with profound astonishment at us. They could scarcely believe that we had eluded all the precautions taken to effect our capture, although we were visibly before them. They said it was "*Khuda-ki-mirzee,*" the will of God, and I suppose, few will doubt that they were right. The meal being finished, Delafosse and I lay down upon two charpoys, native beds, and the privates upon the floor, and we were soon fast asleep. They woke us up between five and six o'clock, to say that a retainer of their Rajah had come to conduct us to the fort of Moorar Mhow. No clothing was furnished us, though Delafosse borrowed a blanket from the zemindar to cover his nakedness. The walking was exquisite torture, from the condition of our feet, and our progress was dilatory indeed till about half way, when guides met us with an elephant and pony. Sullivan and

Murphy were suffering so much from their wounds that we gave them the elephant, and Delafosse and I bestrode the pony. The relief afforded by the quiet all around us, and by the returning sense of security, no words could describe. We passed through several villages, in which our story had preceded us, and the ryots came out with milk and sweetmeats, of which we thankfully partook. Buffalo's milk and native sweets were truly delicious fare.

Night had set in when we reached the residence of Dirigbijah Singh. The Rajah, a venerable old man, was sitting out of doors, surrounded by his retainers; his *vakeel* was at his right; his two sons close at hand, and his bodyguard, armed with swords, shields, and matchlocks. The whole group formed a most picturesque scene, as lighted. up by the attendant torchbearers; they were altogether a strictly oriental company of about a hundred and fifty in number. The pony and elephant having been brought into the center, we alighted and salaamed to the Rajah. He had the whole tale of the siege narrated to him by us, asked after our respective rank in the army, and, having expressed great admiration at our doings, ordered us a supper, with abundance of native wine, assured us of our safety, promised hospitality, and had us shown to our apartment. All the domestic arrangements were in strictly native order, so that they had no beds to spare for us; it must be remembered that our touch would have defiled them forever; they provided us with straw to lie upon, and gave us a sutringee each, a piece of carpet, to cover our bodies. O, that night's rest! Thankful, but weary were we: amid many thoughts that chased each other through my distracted brain, I remember one ludicrously vivid; it was this: how excellent an investment that guinea had proved which I spent a year or two before at the baths in Holborn, learning to swim! And then the straw upon which we lay, though only fit for a pauper's bed in the vagrant ward of some English workhouse, it was to us welcome as the choicest down. In the morning a *hukeem*, native doctor, was sent to dress our wounds; Sullivan and Murphy were suffering greatly; my back and thigh were comparatively well, but the recent crack in the skull was acutely painful. Marvelous to say, Delafosse had not received a single wound. The doctor applied nim leaf poultices, a very favorite recipe with the native leeches, but I found them so desperately irritating that I declined a second application of the kind. The native tailor came also, by the Rajah's directions, and furnished us with trousers and coat each of native cut; and when Hindustani shoes were added to our toilet, we felt quite respectable again. Our host asked us how often we should like our meals. And he kindly arranged for us to have breakfast, luncheon, and a late dinner each day; a great thing for a native house to accomplish, as the Brahmins, to whose company our friend belonged, only cook once a day, and all the feeding for the twenty four hours is done with them at midday. The supplies they gave us were good, consisting of dhal, chupatties, rice, and milk; twice during the month we staid at this hospitable residence they gave us kid's meat, the only animal food they touch; and when a Brahmin has performed a pilgrimage to one of their shrines, he eats no animal food at all henceforth. But sweeter than these repasts was the sleep; day after day, and week after week, we indulged in it, as if we had been fed upon opiates. The only interruption we suffered was caused by the immense number of flies, which, attracted by the wounds, occasioned us considerable annoyance.

We were allowed to walk about any where within the fort, but not beyond its sheltering walls, for the whole neighborhood was swarming with rebels. They frequently came inside the fort, and even into our room, armed to the teeth, but they did not dare to molest us, as some of the Rajah's bodyguard were always in attendance upon us when we received company. Many a conversation we had with Sepoys. Some men of the 56th Native Infantry, and others of the 53d Native Infantry, my own regiment, visited us, and talked freely over the state of affairs in general. The most frequent assertion made by them was, that our raj was at an end. I used to tell them they were talking nonsense, for in a short time reinforcements would arrive; seventy or eighty thousand British troops would land in India and turn the tide the old way; "then the muskets you have in your hands," I said, " with the Government mark upon them, will change hands."

"No, no," they said; "the Nana has sent a sower on a camel to Russia for assistance."

I roared with laughter at the suggestion of such an expedition.

"What are you laughing at, Lord Sahib?"

"O, you are not very well up in your geography to talk in that fashion; a camel might as well be sent to England for help."

"The Nana says he has done so."

"Suppose you gain the country, what shall you do with us?"

"The Nana will send you all down to Calcutta and ship you home, and when he has conquered India, he will embark for England and conquer that country."

"Why, you Brahmins will not go to sea, will you?" "O yes; only we shall not cook upon the voyage."

With such canards as these the Bithoor man has imposed upon the imbecile hordes around him; they believe that the Russians are all Mohammedans, and that the armies of the Czar are to liberate the faithful and their land from the yoke of the Feringhees. Another of the Nana's fables is, that certain watermills which were erected by the Company for grinding grain at a fixed charge for the villagers, were implements in the great work of forcible conversion, and that in the said mills pig bone dust was mixed with the flour.

The annexation of Oude was always upon their tongues; they grew energetic in discussing this theme, and said that in consequence of that one act the Company's raj would cease. It is, very remarkable that the old prophecy of the Brahmin pundits, current in India ever since the battle of Plassy, that the Company's raj would last only one hundred years, has been verified, though not in the manner nor in the sense predicted. "What is the Company?" is a question often discussed in the villages, and various and conflicting are the answers that have been promulgated in reply; the most prevalent opinion among the poor, benighted, swarthy subjects of the far reaching rule of the potentates of Leadenhall street, having been that the said Company was a nondescript brute, that swayed their destinies with a resistless scepter; its species, genus, habitat, all unknown, but only: "Monstrum horrendum, informe, ingens, cui lumen ademptum."

Three times, during our stay at Moorar Mhow, the Nana sent down to our friendly protector, ordering him to surrender our persons. A sower of the 2d Cavalry, and some Sepoys of the 56th Native Infantry, brought the demand; the last came into our apartment, had a chat with us, and asked us how we managed to escape. Our generous old host was deaf to all their persuasions and threats, and sent back word that he was a tributary to the King of Oude, and knew nothing of the Nana's raj. If Nana, Azimoolah & Co. had not had more important business in hand, they would have certainly attacked our refuge, rather than have allowed one relic of the Cawnpore garrison to escape alive; but there is this charm about thackoor hospitality, once claimed, it is not to be dishonored by a trifle.

News from Lucknow occasionally reached us, though by no means so reliable as the graphic communications of that prince of correspondents, the worthy Mr. Russell; for instance, we were told that the Muchee Bhowan had blown up with two hundred Europeans in it. One day the Pnnjaub was lost; another day Madras and Bombay were gone into mutiny; then a hundred thousand Sikhs were said to be marching south to exterminate the English. Our informants believed for themselves all these rumors, and, in fact, it was by such fictions that their wily leaders maintained the hold they had upon them.

Every day the Rajah came to pay us a visit and talk with us kindly, and he often told us that as soon as the adjacent country was quiet, he would forward us to Allahabad.

Much amusement was afforded us by seeing the daily

performance of the devotions of this rigid Brahmin. A little temple detached from the residence was the sphere of operation. The priest, Khangee Loll by name, used to go first and prepare the offerings; divesting himself of his shoes at the temple door, he walked in, and arranged beautiful flowers which had been plucked with the dew upon them, and deposited at the threshold by attendant Brahmins. All round the offerings these floral decorations were arranged with admirable effect in relation to their various hues.

When the Rajah and his two sons made their entry, the shasters were taken out: all four of the worshipers intoned portions of these writings amid the tinkling of bells by the priest. After this, water from the Ganges was poured upon the flowers, and the daily service was complete.

The Ranee often inquired after us by means of messengers. We never saw her ladyship, but the attendants told us that the venetians of her apartments were not impenetrably opaque from within, and that the old lady had seen us, and was concerned for our welfare. Nothing that could contribute to our comfort escaped the kind and minute thoughtfulness of Dirigbijah Singh. I wish he could read English, and peruse my humble effort to express the gratitude I owe to him.

After we had been three weeks at Moorar Mhow, petted in this way by its generous proprietor, the tidings came that a steamer had gone up the Ganges. This was a vessel sent up by General Havelock from Allahabad to explore in the Cawnpore region. In consequence of this, and because a native who had been in the service of the railroad told him that if he did not make arrangements to send us away, our stay might be interpreted into a forcible detention, the Rajah had us conveyed down to a little hamlet within his territory, on the banks of the river. An elephant, escorted by a guard, conveyed us thither at night; the parting was quiet, in order that the attention of the rebels in the neighborhood might not be excited. With abundant expressions of thanks, and some regret, we said farewell to the old brick. I am enabled, with sincere gratification, to add, that Dirigbijah Singh's claims upon the gratitude of the Government of India have not been overlooked; and his loyalty to the Company at a time when almost the whole of Oude was in rebellion, and his generosity to us, poor, friendless refugees, have met with the well deserved recognition of a handsome pension. "May his shadow never be less!"

Our residence at the little hut on the bank of the river was one of the strictest seclusion. Provisions were brought to us twice a day, and a native guard was posted at the door. One day the sentry told us that all kinds of European furniture and papers were floating down the river, and, at my request, he went to the ghaut to see if he could catch anything, and presently returned with a volume bearing the well known inscription, "53d Regiment, Native Infantry Book Club." This was all he could get of the debris of houses, library, and offices, but it was enough to indicate the extent of the destruction effected by the rebels when the recapture of Cawnpore by General Havelock was impending. After remaining five or six days in our retreat, the Rajah came to us, and said, as no more steamers appeared to be going up the river, he had made arrangements to convey us, on the morrow, to a friendly zemindar, who lived in the neighborhood of Futtehpore, and who had engaged to take measures for our safe conduct to the nearest European encampment.

Accordingly, the next morning we were ferried across the river, and escorted to our new host. When we approached the zemindar, he held out his hand with a rupee upon the palm, the native intimation of fidelity to the state. We touched the coin, and the covenant of hospitality was thus in simple formality settled. The old Rajah of Moorah Mhow had evidently provided for our safety and comfort, as nothing was omitted in these new quarters that could conduce to either. On the morning of the third day after crossing from Oude, a bullock hackery was drawn up to the zemindar's hut, and escorted by four of his men, we were driven in the direction of Allahabad. It was a cross country road, and our vehicle was innocent of all springs; but we were at last on the way to our own flag, and not by any means in a state of mind to indulge in complaints or criticisms. After four or five miles of jolting, the native driver, in great alarm, said there were guns planted in the road; we looked ahead, but for some time saw no troops. In a short time an English sentry appeared in view, and I walked up to him. Upon his giving the challenge, I told him we wished to be taken to his commanding officer. Our bronzed countenances, grim beards, huge turbans, and tout ensemble caused them to take us for a party of Afghans. However, Murphy soon recognized some of his old comrades of the 84th; and they greeted us with a truly British cheer, though for a long time dubious of our statement that we had escaped from the massacre of Cawnpore. We were speedily introduced to the officers of the party, which proved to be a detachment, consisting of part of the 84th Regiment and half of Olphert's battery, going up to Cawnpore. Lieutenant, now Captain Woolhouse, of the 84th; Captain Young, of the 4th Native Infantry; and Lieutenant Smithett, of Olphert's battery, gave us a hearty reception. The whole camp was impatient for our story, and we equally impatient to partake of English fare. Never was the beer of our country more welcome; and that first meal, interspersed with a fire of cross questioning about the siege and our subsequent history, inquiries after lost comrades and relatives, and occasional hints at the masquerade style of our accouterment, made a strangely mingled scene of congratulation, humor, lamentation, and good will. Our hunger appeased, the best arrangements possible were made for our comfort. Captain Woolhouse gave me a share of his wagon; Captain Young contributed from his wardrobe; Lieutenant Smithett shared his creature comforts with Delafosse. Sullivan and Murphy were dealt with in like manner by the noncommissioned officers and privates, and the exceeding kindness of the whole company was brought to bear upon our forlorn and indigent condition. Captain Woolhouse's servant shaved my head all round the wound, and the surgeon's dresser of the 84th bound it up.

The detachment we had joined was in Havelock's rear, and about thirty miles from Cawnpore, so that we were once more on the road to the center of the war and the site of our old calamities. As we passed along the way, we often saw the bodies of natives hanging to the trees, sometimes two or three, and in one instance seven hanging to one tree, in various stages of destruction from jackals and vultures. These were criminals who had been executed by the General's order; one of them for attempting to sell poisoned liquor to the troops, others in consequence of having been identified as mutinous Sepoys.

The traces of the General's battles were strewn on all

sides of our route, pieces of gun carriages, remains of hastily improvised intrenchments; and in one village there were a couple of the enemy's guns, which had been taken and left behind spiked. While upon the march, letters were received by Captain Woolhouse from General Neill, warning him to keep a good look out, as the enemy's cavalry were reported to be close to the road on the left side; several alarms were given, but no attack upon us was made.

In one of the villages some of the 84th men had strayed, and while engaged in some expedition which involved their own personal advantage, they caught sight of some horsemen, and panic stricken they returned, shouting, "The cavalry are coming." The column was halted, further inquiries made, and the formidable foe proved to be some *syces* on the Government post horses who had decamped, fearing that the foragers would steal their cattle.

In three days after joining Captain Woolhouse, we reentered Cawnpore. When we came in sight of the old intrenched position, I went off to survey each well remembered post of anxious observation. Where we had left parched and sunburnt ground, covered with round shot, fragments of shell and grape, the grass was now luxuriantly thick. It seemed as though nature had been anxious to conceal the earth's face, and shut out as far as possible the traces of the sufferings caused by some, and endured by others of her sons. It was early morning when I went alone and pondered over that silent well, and its unutterable memories. Fragments of Sepoy skeletons were kicked up by the feet here and there, while the walls of the barracks were pitted and scored all over with shot marks. There was not a square yard in either of the buildings free from the scars of shot. I went in the same solitude all round the principal posts of the enemy, the mess house, and the church, where a few weeks before I had seen hundreds of natives swarming around us in the hope of compassing the destruction of every European life there. Many times afterward I paced the same position, but never with the emotions of that first lonely retrospect. Coming up again with the column, I entered with them the new intrenchment which had been made by Lieutenant Russell, of the Engineers, under General Neill. As soon as it got wind that we had arrived, General Neill sent for Lieutenant Delafosse and myself, heard the outlines of our story, and honored us with an invitation to dine with him the same evening. The General appointed Delafosse to assist Major Bruce, whose manifold duties of police presented a fair field for constant occupation, as they involved secret service, executions, raising native police, and the sale of plunder. I was appointed by General Havelock assistant field engineer to his force under Colonel Cremmelin, in the superintendence of works to resist a second attack upon Cawnpore. Captain Woolhouse, our generous benefactor and friend, went with Havelock to Lucknow, and lost an arm there; he was the only officer who survived amputation in that campaign. One of the earliest casualties after our arrival was the death of Captain Young, who had served under Havelock in Persia, had followed him to Cawnpore as a volunteer, and was now occupied in raising police at Futtehpore, a most hazardous service, as he was alone in the midst of an excited multitude of natives. He dined with General Neill, went to sleep in Colonel Olphert's tent, and died of cholera the next morning. This officer was, as well as a thorough soldier, a most accomplished linguist, and was famous for that rare attainment among Europeans, his most exquisite Persian writing.

My familiarity with the details of the siege introduced me to many an expedition of parties of officers to the melancholy site. I had the honor of pointing out to Generals Neill and Sir Hope Grant, as well as to Captain Layard, of Nineveh celebrity, the chief points of interest, besides accompanying thither brother officers who had lost friends and relatives on that carnage ground.

THE MASSACRE.

Mr. Sharer, the newly appointed magistrate of Cawnpore, who had come up with Havelock's force, exerted himself to the utmost to obtain all possible information respecting the fate of those who had not been shot at the time of embarkation, as well as of the party taken back in Major Vibart's boat from Soorajpore. He had prosecuted most extensive inquiries throughout the native city, and the most reliable accounts which he obtained were in purport as follows:

After the men, who had not escaped in the two boats, had all been shot at the ghaut, the women and children were dragged out of the water into the presence of the Nana, who ordered them to be confined in one of the buildings opposite the Assembly rooms; the Nana himself taking up his residence in the hotel which was close at hand. When Major Vibart's boat was brought back from Soorajpore, that party also was taken into the Nana's presence, and he ordered the men and women to be separated; the former to be shot, and the remainder to join the captives in the dwelling or dungeon beside the hotel. Mrs. Boyes, the wife of Dr. Boyes, of the 2d Cavalry, refused to be separated from her husband; other ladies of the party resisted, but were forcibly torn away, a work of not much difficulty when their wounded, famished state is considered. All the efforts, however, of the Sepoys to sever Mrs. Boyes from her husband were unavailing; they were therefore all drawn up in a line just in front of the Assembly rooms. Captain Seppings asked to be allowed to read prayers; this poor indulgence was given; they shook hands with one another, and the Sepoys fired upon them. Those that were not killed by the volley they dispatched with their tulwars. The spy who communicated these facts could not tell what became of the corpses, but there is little doubt they were thrown into the river, that being the native mode of disposing of them. Captain Seppings, Lieutenant Quin, and Dr. Boyes were all the officers that I know certainly to have been of that unhappy number. As I never could gather that Major Vibart or Lieutenant Masters were there, I suspect they died of their wounds while being taken back. The wretched company of women and children now consisted of 210; namely, 163 survivors from the Cawnpore garrison, and 47 refugees from Futtehghur, of whom that Bithoor butcher had murdered all the males except three officers, whose lives he spared for some purpose, but for what it is impossible to say. The captives were fed with only one meal a day of dhal and chupatties, and these of the meanest sort; they had to eat out of earthen pans, and the food was served by menials of the lowest caste, mehter, which in itself was the greatest indignity that easterns could cast upon them.

Aftermath of the Siege of Cawnpore. Soldiers of the 1st Madras Fusiliers seated amongst the remains of the British entrenchment defences to barracks at Cawnpore which General Sir Hugh Massy Wheeler surrendered in June 1857.

They had no furniture, no beds, not even straw to lie down upon, but only coarse bamboo matting of the roughest make. The house in which they were incarcerated had formerly been occupied as the dwelling of a native clerk; it comprised two principal rooms, each about twenty feet long and ten broad, and besides these a number of dark closets rather than rooms, which had been originally intended for the use of native servants; in addition to these, a courtyard, about fifteen yards square, presented the only accommodation for these two hundred most wretched victims of a brutality in comparison with which hereafter the black hole of Calcutta and its sharp but short agonies must sink into insignificance. It is said that during the former part of their captivity, several of them went to the Nana imploring some commiseration with their wretched state, but in vain; and they desisted altogether from such applications in consequence of one of their number having been cruelly ill treated by the brutal soldiery. Closely guarded by armed Sepoys, many of them suffering from wounds, all of them emaciated with scanty food, and deprived of all means of cleanliness, the deep, dark horrors of the prisoners in that dungeon must remain to their full extent unknown, and even unimagined.

The spies, all of them, however, persisted in the

statement, that no indignities were committed upon their virtue; and as far as the most penetrating investigation into their most horrible fate has proceeded, there is reason to hope that one, and only one exception to the bitterest of anguish was allotted to them, immunity from the brutal violence of their captors' worst passions. Fidelity requires that I should allege what appears to me the only reason of their being thus spared. When the siege had terminated, such was the loathsome condition into which, from long destitution and exposure, the fairest and youngest of our women had sunk, that not a Sepoy would have polluted himself with their touch.

The advance of General Havelock, and his attempt to liberate them, brought the crisis of their fate. Azimoolah persuaded the Nana that the General was only marching upon Cawnpore in the hope of rescuing the women and children, and that if they were killed, the British forces would retire, and leave India. All accounts agree in the statement, that the feted, honored guest of the London season of 1854, was the prime instigator in the most foul and bloody massacre of 1857.

On the 18th of July Havelock encountered the Nana's troops at Futtehpore, under Teekah Singh, a resildar of the 2d Cavalry. The valorous chief and his little band totally routed the Sepoys, captured all their guns, and scattered their survivors, in utter confusion, back toward Cawnpore. The marvel of this victory was not so much in success, as in success under such circumstances. Havelock's column had marched twenty four miles that day, and Major Renaud's nineteen miles, under the heat of a July sun. On the 15th of July the British forces were again engaged, with like results, at Pandoo Nuddy: on that day the Nana put all his captives to death. Havelock was then twenty four miles from Cawnpore. On the 16th he fought another action, defeating the Nana in person, after a battle of two hours and a half. On the morning of the 17th General Havelock entered the city, from which the native populace had fled in every direction to the villages adjacent.

Short, but frequent, were the dispatches that marked his triumphant progress along the path of fire. The following is that which he drew breath to pen on the 17th of July:

"By the blessing of God, I recaptured this place yesterday, and totally defeated Nana Sahib in person, taking more than six guns, four of siege caliber. The enemy were strongly posted behind a succession of villages, and obstinately disputed, for the one hundred and forty minutes, every inch of the ground; but I was enabled, by a flank movement to my right, to turn his left, and this gave us the victory. Nana Sahib had barbarously murdered all the captive women and children before the engagement. He has retired to Bithoor, and blew up this morning, on his retreat, the Cawnpore magazine. He is said to be strongly fortified. I have not yet been able to get in the return of the killed and wounded, but estimate my loss at about seventy, chiefly from the fire of grape."

The explosion of the magazine referred to in this dispatch, we heard at Moorar Mhow, a distance of thirty miles, as distinctly as if it had been the firing of a gun in the Rajah's fort.

When Mr. Sherer entered the house of horrors, in which the slaughter of the women had been perpetrated, the rooms were covered with human gore; articles of clothing that had belonged to women and children, collars, combs, shoes, caps, and little round hats, were found steeped in blood; the walls were spattered with blood, the mats on the floor saturated, the plaster sides of the place were scored with sword cuts, and pieces of long hair were all about the room. No writing was upon the walls; and it is supposed that the inscriptions, which soon became numerous, were put there by the troops, to infuriate each other in the work of revenging the atrocities that had been perpetrated there, There is no doubt that the death of the unhappy victims was accomplished by the sword, and that their bodies, stripped of all clothing, were thrown into an adjacent well.

A Bible was found that had belonged to Miss Blair, in which she had written: "27th June. Went to the boats.

29th. Taken out of boats. 30th. Taken to Sevadah Kothi, fatal day."

One officer who was present, wrote, "I picked up a mutilated prayer book; it had lost the cover, but on the flyleaf is written, 'For dearest mamma, from her affectionate Louis, June, 1845.' It appears to me to have been opened on page 36, in the Litany, where I have but little doubt those poor dear creatures sought and found consolation, in that beautiful supplication. It is here sprinkled with blood. The book has lost some pages at the end, and terminates with the 47th Psalm, in which David thanks the Almighty for his signal victories over his enemies."

The only other authentic writings that were left in that den of death were two pieces of paper, bearing the following words. The first was written by one of the Misses Lindsay.

"Mamma died, July 12th, (that is, Mrs. G. Lindsay.)

Alice died, July 9th, (daughter of above.)

George died, June 27th, (Ensign G. Lindsay, 10th N. I.)

Entered the barracks, May 21st.

Cavalry left, June 5th.

First shot tired, June 6th.

Uncle Willy died, June 18th, (Major W. Lindsay.)

Aunt Lilly died, June 17th, (Mrs. W. Lindsay.)

Left barracks, June 27th."

The other, in an unknown hand, ran thus:

"We went into the barracks on the 21st of May. The 2d Cavalry broke out at two o'clock in the morning of the 5 th of June, and the other regiments went off during the day. The next morning, while we were sitting out in front of the barracks, a twenty-four-pounder came flying along and hit the intrenchment, and from that day the firing went on till the 25th of June, when the enemy sent a treaty, which the General agreed to, and on the 27th we all left the B [entrenched barracks] to go down to A [Allahabad] in boats; when we got to the river, the enemy began firing on us, killed all the gentlemen and some of the ladies; set fire to the boats, some were drowned, and we were taken prisoners and taken to a house, put all in one room."

In a native doctor's house there was found a list of the captives, written in Hindee; and from this it appears that a number of the sufferers died from their wounds and from cholera, which broke out in their midst.

Captain Thompson was subsequently appointed to the command of native police in the Cawnpore district. On the 3d of February, 1858, he was severely wounded in an engagement with a body of rebels, on the road to Calpee, and was obliged to submit to hospital life for three weeks, after which he returned on furlough to England.

Finis.

Made in the USA
Middletown, DE
17 January 2020